Thomas Kull

Women
in Shadow and Light

Also by Jan Goff-LaFontaine:

Reflections—Between the Lines: The Healing of the Vietnam Generation
Turner Publishing

Women in Shadow and Light

Journeys from Abuse to Healing

EDITED AND PHOTOGRAPHED BY

Jan Goff-LaFontaine

WITH A FOREWORD BY
Iyanla Vanzant

Reno, Nevada

Creative Minds Press
an imprint of **Beagle Bay Books**
Reno, Nevada
info@beaglebay.com

Book Design: Robin P. Simonds

Visit our websites at:
http://www.creativemindspress.com
http://www.beaglebay.com

Library of Congress Control Number: 2004116067
ISBN: 0-9749610-5-1

This book is printed on acid-free paper.

First Edition
Printed in China
12 11 10 09 08 07 06 05 — 1 2 3 4 5

Dedication

This book is dedicated to the beautiful women who fill its pages. They shared the most precious gift—their hearts—to offer hope and healing to others.

And to the woman who inspired me and taught me how to be and how to give, Mary Ann, my step-mom.

If you knew what I know about the power of giving, you would not let a single meal pass without sharing it in some way.
—Buddha

Table of Contents

Foreword

When Jan Goff-LaFontaine approached me at the "Women and Power" conference in New York with her book, *Women in Shadow and Light*, I was struck by how much her work resonated with my own experiences of childhood abuse; living in abusive relationships and believing, for so long, that I simply could not take care of myself. Like so many women, during my most difficult times I was tempted to give up. But instead, I held on and can now say that my experiences have given me profound insight into my self and life. From our deepest places of pain we experience intense growth. From the most vile and violent expressions of anger come love and compassion. If we believe we are not powerful; if we believe we are not capable; if we believe we are not worthy; this will determine how we respond to the situations and circumstances of our lives.

This takes a courage and strength that many women are not always aware we have. The forty women in this book have learned that they do. They, too, have suffered indignities and violence at the hands of others. Their diversity attests to that fact that violence against women does not discriminate by age, race or social status, and could happen to any of us.

Whether it is at a kitchen table, on a park bench or from the driver's seat in a mini van, women tell stories about themselves and their lives. They tell stories that heal themselves and other women. They tell stories that teach lessons. *Women In Shadow and Light* tells their stories so that we may all learn the lessons of healing. Like myself, these women are living proof that it is not what happens to us that creates our reality, but how we choose to respond that determines whether we live a life of anger or one of joy. Each of us must come to the recognition that the very experiences appearing as obstacles were actually pointing us toward our purpose. This awareness may feel impossible, even ridiculous when someone is violently beating you, emotionally demoralizing you or sexually abusing you. Yet, each woman in a "shadow" must come to realize that only *she* has the power to move herself toward the "light." Change is an inside job and is the only power required to transform a life.

When you take control—walk away; dare to start anew—you reclaim your power. You give yourself permission to create a better life. And creating a better life will enable you to create a better community and a better world.

Being human presents us with many challenges, and when we share some of this burden with others it helps to lighten our load. As these women share with us their journeys, we all become one, and in that oneness we are all strengthened and encouraged. We know that we all share with them the quest for spiritual strength and joy. The first step in that quest is often being honest—with ourselves as well as others. Once we tell ourselves the truth, we can let go of a painful past and open ourselves to our purpose. These women have taken a courageous leap of faith in their decision to be honest to the world in a very public way. Allowing themselves to be vulnerable in this way has revealed their incredible strength. They have overcome the feelings of self-doubt and worthlessness that stole their dreams for so many years while they were in abusive situations. They have broken free of the bonds of fear that held them down. They come to us with love: Love for themselves, and for all the other women who at this very moment need to hear their truths.

There is nothing more powerful than women coming together in an environment of loving support and focusing their intention on helping each other and all other women to heal. Jan Goff-LaFontaine has facilitated this kind of healing circle with these forty women, many of whom have never met, but still feel a strong bond. She has created the potential for these women to become healers as they bring their message of hope and love into the world through this book.

Both in the words of these women, and in the portraits Jan has created with them, we can feel this love. We can see their light and their inner beauty. The women in this book make a statement of hope that echoes my message. To these women, and to all who read this book—This is your time. The power is in your hands. Stand in your shoes, and dance your dance. Find your voice and sing your song. The reason you are on this planet is to awaken your god-self, to celebrate life and to do what brings you joy! And remember, you are always free to choose. Choose joy!

Be Blessed!

Rev. Iyanla Vanzant, Author
Founder of Inner Visions Institute for Spiritual Development
Life Coach on NBC's *Starting Over*

Acknowledgments

My deepest gratitude to all the women who shared their hearts with me to make this book. You are all amazing and beautiful, and your journeys are engraved in my heart forever.

Special thanks and love to my dear friend, Sheila, for being my partner in this project from Day One. For the creation of the performance, the endless hours of transcribing, planning, deciding, worrying, and working; for keeping me organized, keeping me sane and keeping me laughing. It meant so much to share it all with you.

Huge thanks to everyone at HELP of Door County for your endless support from the very beginning. Allin, Cindy and Barb were my lifelines so many times I lost count. This would not be happening without you.

Endless thanks to my husband Roger, for his tireless support, and being open to learn and grow from this project. Love keeps me afloat.

My sincere appreciation to Kathleen, Katie and Antonia for your help in transcribing tapes.

Thanks to my good friend, Dee, for the creation of my website, for your endless patience when I made changes, and for still being my friend when it was all done.

Merci to Loretta for your editing help and for making me take a break when I needed it, but didn't know it.

Katie, thanks for all your great ideas and help, and for jumping into this before you ever even met me. Thanks for coming to New York and for letting me watch you grow into your power.

Thanks and love to Brooke for photographing our performance, and for sharing your journey with me.

Thanks to all the people who offered support, advice, and a safe and sacred space for photographing these beautiful women: Julia Bresnahan, Jan Comstock, Rich and Dorothy Burkhardt, Cheri Ault and Dick Bartlett, Kathy Navis.

Thanks to Dan Anderson and Donna Brown for production help and valuable advice.

Thanks to Michele Geiger-Bronsky for cookies and the salon.

Thank you Kevin and Suzie Osborne and Ernie Stolle for your heartfelt technical assistance.

My gratitude to Iyanla Vanzant for the inspiration she offered me at the Women and Power conference, and for being willing to share her joy and inspiration in the foreword of this book.

Thanks to Elizabeth Lesser for gathering such an amazing group of women at the Women and Power conference, and for taking the time to share your feelings about my book.

Thank you to Ellen Bass, my fellow Santa Cruzan, for sharing your knowledge and feelings about my book.

Much gratitude to Mary Ann and the women of the Fresh Start Program for the inspiration to do this.

Many thanks to Peninsula Arts Association and Wisconsin Arts Board for the support and grants that helped get me here.

Thanks to Irene, Lena, and everyone at the Fairfield Art Museum for taking a chance, and for supporting me with the exhibit.

Thank you to Bay Photo Labs and Peninsula Imaging for your generosity in processing my film.

Thanks to Tom Soik for all your time, work and caring about this project.

Thanks to Peninsula Art School for many hours in your great darkroom.

Many thanks to my publishers for your belief in me and your enthusiasm for this project. And for stress relief when I need it.

Women
in Shadow and Light

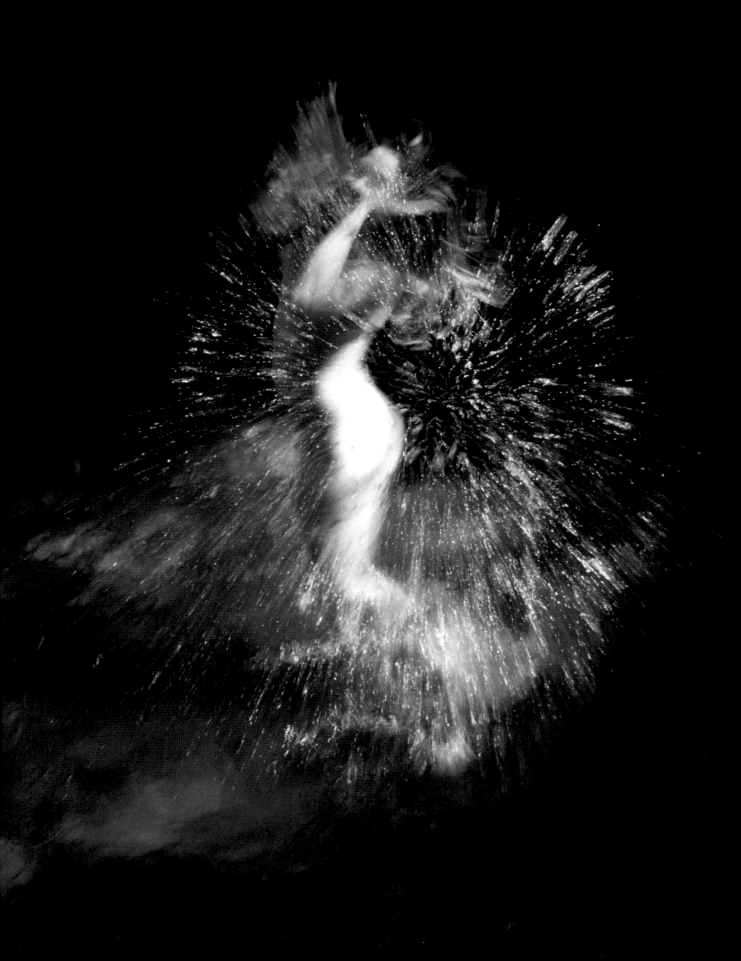

Speaking Out

"Trusting another person with my story and seeing that they won't use it against me is a huge leap for me. I'm thankful to all the courageous women who are part of this project. Their courage showed me that I, too, can heal, and be a strong woman."—Milli

Many people ask why I decided to do this book, and how a book on abuse survivors can be about celebration and joy. The short answer is, my background as a social worker and the powerful influence of my step-mom, gave me a deep desire to do something that could make a difference in women's lives. And after sharing the trauma as well as the triumph of friends who have been abused, I wanted to make the book a celebration of the strength and beauty of women; a reclaiming of their own joy and a gift of hope to others.

As the project unfolded though, I felt other reasons were stirring; something in me searching for expression. Frequently, we offer to others what we most need to learn, and my writing constantly guides me to new truths. Perhaps it was my own healing I sought as I began my journey with these women of courage.

When I was six years old, I was walking home from a friend's house, just two grassy, picket-fenced yards from where I lived. A man pulled up to the curb and asked directions, so I went up to the open window of his '53 Chevy. He was young, with reddish blond hair, and had a big friendly smile. When I got to his window, I saw that he had his erect penis (although I didn't know it was called a penis then) in his rapidly moving hand. His friendly smile turned to a frightening guttural laugh. I screamed and ran home faster than I knew my short skinny legs could go. I was in tears as I burst through the screen door, blurting out what I saw as my mother held my sobbing little body tightly and my dad ran out to look for him. I remember two policemen coming into our living room and asking me questions, my mom still holding onto me, as if she could protect me from the evil outside our door. As I write this, fifty years later, I feel my heartbeat quicken, my stomach tighten, the fear of an innocent child welling up in my body.

I don't think of this incident often; before this book, I wasn't even aware it was still in my memory. But suddenly there it was—a big Technicolor image pounding at the door of my mind. He didn't even touch me—but his face and his car and his penis made an indelible mark on me all the same. I didn't know until I was researching this book that what he did is called sexual assault.

This memory also pushed to the surface other events I had dismissed as insignificant or embarrassing, or my own fault. I felt the same emotions other women in the book feel as I allowed myself to admit there was a time in my own marriage that felt abusive; my husband's long-repressed guilt and anger over Vietnam boiled over and caused us both a great deal of pain. We healed with the help of others in similar situations willing to share their experiences. Now I could hold out a hand to other women in the same way.

As I interviewed the women in this book, they gave me permission to allow the shadow areas of my own past into the light. These women also moved my niece, who is the closest I will ever come to having a daughter, to begin healing from her long-repressed memories of rape. My vision of helping other women had suddenly become very personal, and a desire to continue this work became my mission. This helped me to realize that we *all* bear the scars of some kind of assault or abuse. Violence against women of all ages is such an insidious social issue that we are all touched by it. We are so deeply connected to each other as human beings, that what happens to one, affects us all. The women who fill these pages could be any of us—or our daughters or girlfriends, our nieces or neighbors, our mothers or wives.

They are Everywoman.

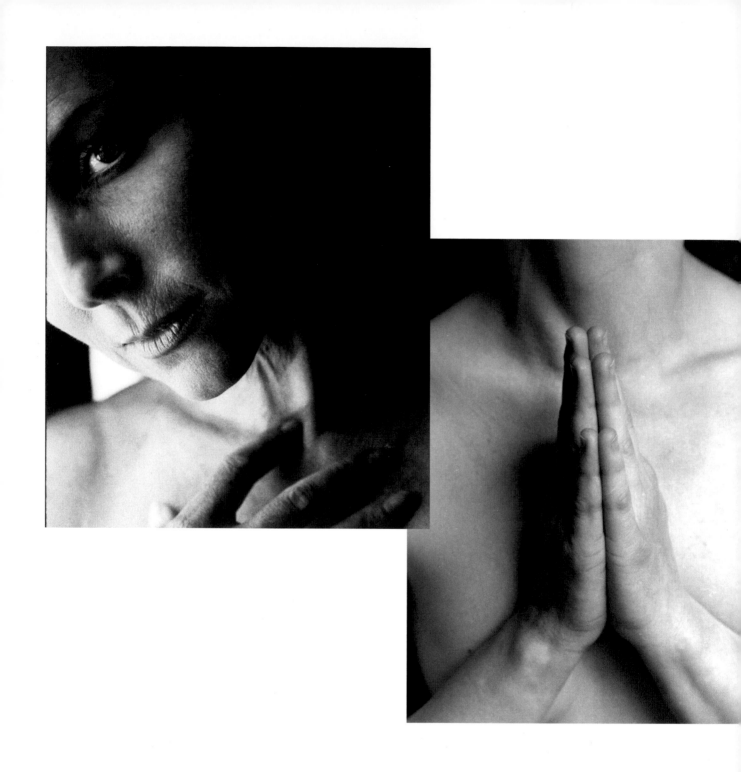

Everywoman

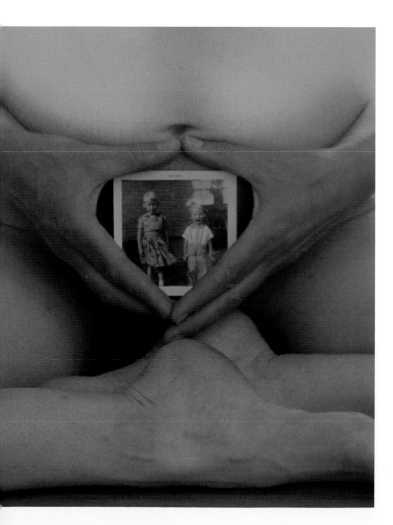

A composite of three different women, Everywoman comes together to represent all women. She is flesh and bone, head and heart, hands and hips: all the parts that at once make us all the same and allow each of us to be unique. Like the rest of the women in this book, she could be any one of us—and truly she is all of us. She was ripped apart, her pieces scattered, yet now she emerges stronger at the broken places; she is whole, reinvented, born anew.

Everywoman comes out of the shadows with an unwavering gaze, looking us in the eye, daring us to look back at her, and not turn away.

Do her hands protect her heart or quietly invite us in? Do they pray, meditate, plead with us to listen, offer comfort?

Everywoman is strong, set on a solid foundation that she alone has built. Does she cover yesterday's memory, or is she bringing it out into the light to see it for the first time?

Everywoman has parts of her that can feel small and vulnerable, angry and afraid. But as one hand reaches out to touch another, Everywoman gathers the pieces, and once again celebrates a strength born of vulnerability, beauty radiating from within and an unshakeable courage.

Visions of Healing

"Even if you only tell your story to one person, you are claiming your inner power, letting go of shame, and not allowing what happened to define who you are."—Katie

The women in this book offered me a precious gift: the opportunity to be a part of their healing. They allowed themselves to be vulnerable, trusting me with their most tender emotions, their deepest feelings and often their darkest secrets. They honored me by allowing me to share their journey, to hold their delicate spirit in my hands for that moment. They shared their dreams and opened themselves to an avenue of healing they had never imagined as we worked together to create their very personal portrait.

The inspiration for the portraits came from a dear friend of mine who was in an abusive relationship for many years. Twenty years later, Margaret still hears his voice telling her "You'll never leave me; you have an ugly body and little tits, and no other man will want you." I thought about how his mental abuse lingered twenty years after she left the physical beatings behind. I reflected on how the media images of supermodels influence staggering numbers of women who have eating disorders and low self-esteem because they don't have what our society deems the "perfect body." I began to understand how this body image issue is compounded for women whose bodies and minds have been violated by abuse. Some look at their bodies as ugly, evil or shameful. Many use weight gain as a means of protection, a way to ward off the attention of men who might hurt them. The question haunting me was: how can we change our perception—and even influence society's concept—of what it means to be a beautiful woman? My vision was to allow each of the women to help create her own portrait in order to see her body in a new way; to see it as beautiful and precious. To see it as a work of art.

One of the questions asked in each woman's interview was, "In what part of your body did you began to feel healing?" This often became one of the keys to creating her photograph. For one woman, the photograph revolved around her chest, because she said that when she left her abusive marriage, she could finally breathe. Another said she could now see clearly, so her portrait focused on her eyes. This and other questions about what helped her to heal allowed each woman to create her portrait as her personal symbol of healing. The interview helped peel away the layers of shame and pain until only the blank canvas of her body remained. On this, she could portray her essence.

By the time the interview process was completed, the women—no matter what their age, size or shape—did not hesitate to remove that last wall of defense that clothing offers. Most found the experience of using their bodies as an expression of healing to be freeing and empowering. One woman, Jeanne, put it this way, "The interview was really the naked part for me; sharing that very vulnerable part of me was terrifying. The photograph was an integral part of the healing process. To have someone photograph me in beautiful surroundings, filled with lovely natural light, and interested in creating from my shape a beautiful composition . . . well, for the first time in years, I actually felt beautiful. When I look at the photograph I feel peaceful and strong."

Beautiful, peaceful, strong. This is her vision, her redefined self-image. Each of these women has transformed her life, moving far beyond the role of victim to see in herself the strength and beauty that was always there. They are recreating themselves, and they implore society to take a closer look, to see what the meaning of beauty truly is. They feel empowered, as they hold out hope to help others find healing.

Photo by Brooke E. Schneider

Once Upon A Time . . .

"I'd like to hold out hope to other women . . . to let them know they aren't alone; they aren't the only ones these things happened to, and they can survive."—Ellie

In the idyllic land of Door County, Wisconsin, far away from the crime and violence of big cities, is where this tale began. This peninsula in Lake Michigan, dubbed "the Cape Cod of the Midwest," is filled with farmland, tiny towns and extraordinary artists. Everyone knows everyone, and no one locks their door.

But behind those doors, violence against women and girls happens as much as it does in any city. It's just that no one knew, and no one talked about it . . . until the summer of 2003.

That was when the women of Door County decided to reclaim their power, their bodies and their lives. It was when they realized that being safe doesn't mean hiding in shame; it means speaking out. And that being beautiful isn't about looking like a supermodel; it's just allowing who they are on the inside to shine through. It was when these women decided to step out of the shadows and into the spotlight to tell everyone what went on behind the doors of Door County.

When the idea for this project first began rumbling around in my heart, I asked my good friend Sheila Sarey-Saperstein what she thought of it. I knew she was a domestic violence survivor, and wondered what her reaction would be. Would she, or any other woman in Door County, be willing to go public with her hidden past? What would she think of my idea for the portraits? Mostly, would she be brave enough to be the first one to step forward?

Sheila is a photographer herself. She is educated, vibrant, outgoing—and one of my best friends. I felt that if she weren't willing, no one else would be. Sheila's response was a characteristic explosion of enthusiasm. She not only agreed to be my first subject, but also my partner in creating what would become the *Out of the Shadows* photographic exhibit.

The next week, I went to an art opening, and with typical small-town serendipity, I met the coordinator of a domestic violence agency called HELP. Cindy would become my next subject, and also be instrumental in referring many of the other women who participated. Once we established this alliance with HELP, the project seemed to move into fast-forward. That is when I knew I was doing the work I was supposed to be doing.

We received a grant from the local arts association that would take the project in a new direction. I wanted to interview women all over the country, and eventually did, but the grant stipulated that it be used only to interview women who lived in Door County. What I initially perceived as a limitation created an entirely different, and ultimately more powerful, approach for the project. It opened the eyes and hearts of a community to see beyond its outward beauty, to the pain beneath the shiny surface. Since the first twenty women I interviewed lived in the same community, we were able to come together on several occasions, and a bond developed. The camaraderie added a new dimension, allowing a larger impact on themselves and their community, and opening doors for others to speak about the unspeakable.

Sheila's theater background, combined with the growing connection among the women, led us to a decision to add a performance component to the exhibit. This was something I never would have imagined, but it became another important step in healing.

We were uncertain if any of the women would want to participate in a performance, but we put the idea out. We were surprised when over half the women gave enthusiastic thumbs up, and the performance began to take shape. Some women wanted to write poems about their healing, some decided to do music or dance. All would participate in an emotionally revealing and empowering exercise we called tone poems.

Gayle, one of the women I interviewed, put together a kind of fill-in-the-blank exercise based on common threads I noticed in every interview. They were titled "Shame," "My Body" and "You." Every woman I interviewed carried shame and guilt about her abuse, had body image issues, and strong feelings about the perpetrator (You). These were the issues we wanted to address together.

We all gathered one evening, with plenty of chocolate and other comfort food. We filled out the sheets Gayle gave us with one or two word answers, then put them all in a pile and passed them out so no one would read her own. The exercise required spontaneous answers, and knowing it would be anonymous allowed everyone to feel free to express her deepest feelings. Every woman was able to walk in someone else's shoes as she read their responses, and she could also to hear her own words in someone else's voice. It was extremely powerful, and we all agreed it had to be part of the performance.

Gayle offered to put everyone's answers together into the tone poems we would read as a group during the performance. I didn't know how she would do this, but decided to trust the process, and let it go. This became almost a mantra for me as I saw things happening with this project that I had never imagined possible. Instead of trying to make things happen the way I wanted, as I have been known to do, I just got out of the way and allowed it to take shape. I realized it was no longer *my* project; it now belonged to the women who *were* the project, and I was happy to just drive the bus and turn where they told me to.

I was fortunate to exhibit at the Fairfield Art Museum, perhaps the most prestigious venue in Door County. This community is very supportive of the arts, but art usually means the beautiful side of life: the flowers, barns and lighthouses that grace the countryside. So I knew it was a risk for the Fairfield to show my work. The subject was one no one talks about, and there was some nudity—which always has the possibility of being controversial, especially when it's your neighbor.

The exhibit was one of the most talked about and well-attended they have ever had. The opening was packed and the air was electric. There were tears and hugs and a huge outpouring of respect and support from the community. Watching as women saw their portraits for the first time, and seeing them watch as others saw their image and read their story was an experience none of us will forget. Three of the women who'd chosen to use pseudonyms came to me at the end of the night and said they would like to use their real names. They were astounded that they'd shared their dark secret and no one turned away. This support allowed them to own their story, to embrace their shadows as part of what shaped them. By the time the book was finished only four of the forty women chose to use pseudonyms.

The next week there was another reception—for the performance. We had one rehearsal the night before—and it was a complete disaster. It was the first time I really had an idea of what this performance Sheila had talked about would look like, and I have to say it wasn't good. But I knew how important this was. It took immeasurable courage for these women to bare their souls and their bodies with me to create this exhibit. Now they were going one giant leap beyond that to stand up in front of their community and share their hearts. It's hard for most people to speak in public at all, but to speak publicly about matters so private, with words that have never been spoken before, seemed almost heroic to me.

We arrived an hour early to organize, getting more nervous as we saw the gallery filling to capacity again. One last group hug and we were on. The performance went flawlessly except for me trying to turn on music for a dancer; but even that seemed okay, as people laughed and lightened the mood a bit. My body tingled with goose bumps the entire night, as one woman after another shared her pain and her power and her healing. These were not actresses, but real women sharing their once-broken hearts. At the end, one of the women, Jeanne, sang *The Rose*. The other women stood in front of her as one, arms wrapped around each other. I heard one voice, then a few more, then the entire audience, singing along softly. Every man and woman there embraced all of us, eyes glistening with tears for our pain and our joys—human hearts connecting to one another.

Several of the women told me later their sharing had been so deep it brought them back to their abusive experience and their nightmares. It made me realize the healing process is not linear, but is a continuous journey, with many peaks and valleys. Yet when they were invited to do the performance again the next month, none of them hesitated. They had seen men, along with the women in the audience, shedding tears. They knew how deeply their sharing would affect others, and how much awareness they were creating, and how many other women would know they weren't alone. So they did it again. And again. And they will continue to do it because it might help even one person each time they open their hearts to share. The shadows of their past can help someone else see the light.

So much has happened that I never could have dreamed, and the work has truly taken on a life of its own. There has been a great deal of healing, and some tears, but also plenty of laughter and fun. The women have found that being able to express their healing through nude portraits has been an empowering experience for them, but it also made for some grand adventures and fits of giggles. These were not studio portraits, so trying to find a place private enough for the women to feel comfortable was often challenging. We found ourselves photographing in such diverse places as a campground, a courthouse mediation room, a very cold lake, a very hot yoga studio, climbing a tree, lounging on boulders and in a New York City hotel room. As Gayle said to me, "Being able to laugh in the nude! What a concept for me, after hiding for all of those years." The making of each photograph was a moment I, and I'm sure each of them, will always cherish.

The interviews moved beyond Door County to include women from every corner of the country, of all ages, and from diverse racial and economic groups. Even though the branches of this beautiful tree have grown in many directions, it is deeply rooted in Door County. Lives have changed because of this, and the women are eager to help others do the same. Someone who saw the exhibit asked us to make a video that can be used by agencies and women's groups everywhere. During the taping it was exciting to hear the women speak of their healing and growth, exuding a confidence that wasn't there the first time I interviewed them. They have become advocates, doing public speaking, and reaching out to others at every opportunity. The wounded have become healers.

The women in this book have woven together the shadows with the light, wrapped themselves in the fabric of their lives, and found their way back to the beautiful and extraordinary woman they always were.

Cheryl

"I'm amazed how the image of offering a flower in my hands emerged, because a friend said I was like a flower with a rock on it, just starting to bloom. My vision of healing is to be very warm, especially my hands."

Her father began forcing her to masturbate him and do other sexual acts before she was four years old, always telling her it was her fault.

"My father blamed my hands, like I made him have an erection, and now I had to make it go away. As a little girl, I'd look at them and say 'Bad hands!' When I finally had the courage to say no to my father at age seven, he raped me, holding my hands behind my back, and I bled so much I almost died. So now, anytime I speak up for myself, my hands get cold."

He said he'd kill her if she told, so she shut down, not letting herself feel or remember anything. But eight years ago, memories began to resurface.

"It happened during a Feldenkrais session, and the memories came out almost violently in my body. My family wanted to deny it and it was very difficult for all of us. When it was a secret, I was able to pretend he never did this, but. Now I've confronted him, and he's agreed to meet with a mediator. It's hard to admit, but I do want a relationship with my dad.

"I need to forgive myself for being a victim. Connecting with my inner voice through prayer and meditation has helped me heal. If I want to live fully I have to exercise more of the strength I know I have. Like speaking up and not turning cold. It's such a gift to be part of this, and be able to speak up without fear."

Post Interview Letter:

Dear Jan,

Thank you so much for a very special experience. Your work is so beautifully transforming to all who come in contact with it, and it has had a tremendous impact on my healing in so many ways. It was healing for me to tell a stranger what happened to me and to *not* have my fears confirmed—that I would be ostracized, hurt or disgraced for sharing my true experience. Exposing it publicly is another big healing step. The next was meeting with my father.

We met with a mediator and I told him all the ways I forgive him, defining it for myself and for him. I told him that I saw him as a whole person capable of beneficial and harmful acts, that I listen to him with respect, and that I do not tell others what he did to me to bring shame onto him. I said the words "I forgive you."

Cheryl went to live in an ashram in India as the next step in her healing. When she returned for a short time, she wanted to have a meeting with her father where they didn't talk about the abuse. She wrote me again.

I knew I had grown in my heart a great deal and I had the space inside to feel safe and have compassion for him at the same time. As we sat for dinner, I felt my stomach churning as I looked at him. I felt no difference between us. He did things I didn't like, but that I had seen myself do days earlier. So much mirroring between us. I felt a deeper closeness with my own self, and a compassion for him without the idealization I had as a child. When I got back to my friend's house, I went to bed and wept; a deep crying from my womb. I felt I was releasing a feeling of universal pain—one that occurs between fathers and daughters. I can put words to it now, but honestly there were no words then. It was an absolute healing.

I have received a beautiful gift of you listening, and then supporting me in coming up with a photographic image of my healing journey. It helped me to heal some negative feelings about photography related to the abuse. It's truly a gift to be part of this, and to be able to speak up, knowing that my story of courage can inspire others. Instead of feeling small and damaged, I am brave, I have healed, and I am an example of how others can heal, too.

With Love and Gratitude, Cheryl

Crystal Light Shines Through You

No one can stop you from sharing your light
You've always had the power
But now you magnify your own Inner Self
Your heart expands
With love overflowing with courage

The contentment you experience is the fruitful yield
Of your own cultivation
Perseverance, tolerance, self-restraint, firm conviction, steadfastness
All of these qualities

You have delved so deeply
There is no one who can tell you who you are
You know yourself
No question

And now you illumine the world
Your relationships shine with honesty
Lies are for the darkness

Out of the Shadows
No one defines you
Your imperfections are also stellar marks
Refracting the light into diverse colors
You are a crystal
Purified through intense pressure
Now beautifully revealed

Untouchable/Unchangeable/Unending
Infinite.

Shine!
Out of the Shadows
Shine!

Katie

"To me, self-love means valuing my potential, never giving way to fear and becoming strong in who I am. Learning to love myself was one of my greatest struggles, but owning my trauma has transformed me into a pillar of strength and confidence. This has all shaped the beautiful woman I am today."

Katie's first abusive experience was when she was eight. Being raised Methodist, she felt ostracized when she transferred to a Catholic private school.

"I was so happy when I finally made a friend, and went to her house often. But it became a place I dreaded; it was where she molested me. Using that word between two young girls seems strange, but maybe we need to expand our definition of abuse for every story to surface. My truth is that I felt scared, silenced and overpowered; I never told anyone about it for ten years. Today I feel compassion for her; I don't believe a young girl could think to do such things on her own, so an adult probably abused her in similar ways."

But this shaped Katie's view of sex and relationships for many years.

"My first ideas of sexual intimacy were unhealthy, complex and equated with being dominated. Because I never talked about what happened, and never truly felt my body belonged to me, when it came to intimacy, I usually felt like a sex object. The only healthy sexual experience I had was when I lost my virginity to my first love, and felt truly cared for. But my fears of intimacy resurfaced to an even greater degree after I was raped."

Katie attended a female cousin's wedding in Dallas, where her twenty-four-year-old male cousin raped her, and shook her world to the core.

"This was someone I'd loved and trusted; family. He betrayed me, in a violent way. I later learned he'd been in a mental institution and was on Ritalin, but our family is secretive about such things. When I wanted to go to court, my dad convinced my mom and I that a trial would be too hard on me, but I felt partly he did it to avoid conflict in the family. My aunt blamed me for ruining the wedding, and my uncle called me a slut. None of my relatives acknowledged my cousin raped me, let alone tried to console me. We still haven't spoken, eight years later. My mom finally helped me see that I *had* to focus on *me* and my healing, and let go of what anyone else thought. She was afraid she was going to lose me. I was unable to eat or see friends, or go to school; I had low self-esteem, and was very angry. I isolated myself, constantly fearing I could be violated again. The only time I felt safe was with my mom; I just wanted to curl back into her womb."

With the help of her mom, rape crisis counselors, and therapy, Katie began healing. At eighteen she joined a Buddhist peace group, and the next year formed a college group called Sisters Breaking Silence, continuing to heal and grow as she spoke out. But, as too often happens, she was raped again.

"I had worked hard at being able to see sex as a nurturing, empowering expression of love. But that was shattered when I was raped again. I'd just turned twenty-one after my second year in college, and went out to some clubs with a girlfriend. Her boyfriend introduced me to his friend, who later brought me home. He came in for a short time and then I asked him to leave."

She locked the doors and went to bed. But, aroused by their brief encounter, he refused to accept her rejection, breaking into her apartment through a window.

"At six a.m., I awoke to see him in my bedroom doorway, and despite my attempts to stop him, he raped me. But this time I would not be a silent victim. It took a lot of courage, but I went to court with the support of friends and family. The D.A. constantly told me I could quit, but I was determined to stand up for myself. The court valued his perception of what happened more than mine, so he was only convicted of trespassing, and given three years probation. The judge believed me, but thought the way I said 'no' was too mousy, so I learned to roar like a lion. Going to court made me stronger; I stood up for myself and claimed my voice."

In finding her strong clear voice, she developed strength and wisdom beyond her twenty-three years.

"From a place where once my spirit was in pieces, now emerges a wholeness. Out of my sorrow and despair, comes a celebration of my free spirit. From my pain, a sword of strength as solid as my will and tenacity to overcome. I have replaced the word *victim* with *victor.* I know I can confront any obstacle ahead of me; I believe in myself and know who I am. Now I'm focused on growing in my talents as a filmmaker and singer. One of my goals is to deconstruct the way women are depicted as sex objects in media and create empowering images that reflect our confidence, inner-beauty and humanity. In whatever I do, I am dedicated to being a strong role model to women.

"I've learned that it's important to stand in my own shoes, to speak out against any kind of injustice, and turn poison into medicine. I encourage women all over the world to claim their voice and speak up about any trauma in their life no matter how long ago it happened or who the perpetrator was. Even if you only tell your story to one person, you are claiming your inner-power, letting go of shame, and not allowing what happened to define who you are. I will never again suffer in silence and isolation under the false belief that I am to blame for someone else's neurosis and violent behavior. I am more than what has happened to me, I am an artist, a videographer, a singer, a dancer and a lover."

Post Interview Letter:

In the past three months I have grown from a young woman searching for her voice to one who has embraced her inner-power. Beginning my work with Jan and her book, *Women in Shadow and Light*, started a new chapter in my life. While transcribing some of the tapes of women Jan interviewed for the book, I suddenly felt connected to a sisterhood of women, who had once perceived themselves in the same shameful way I had, yet they did not allow themselves to be defined by what had happened to them. Suddenly, the shame I had been holding onto didn't have as much power over me.

I realized I wasn't the first woman to look at myself in the mirror and find it difficult to say *I love you.* Working on this book has changed my perception of my body and helped me claim my voice. Before this experience, I regarded nudity as a moral dilemma, but now I can say it's been one of the most liberating experiences I've had. The trauma of rape is never fully healed; we carry the memory of the abuse in our bodies, so being able to feel free and confident in my body again has been an empowering transformation.

Hearing these women speak of their worst nightmares from the most unbridled honest place in their heart has forever changed my life.

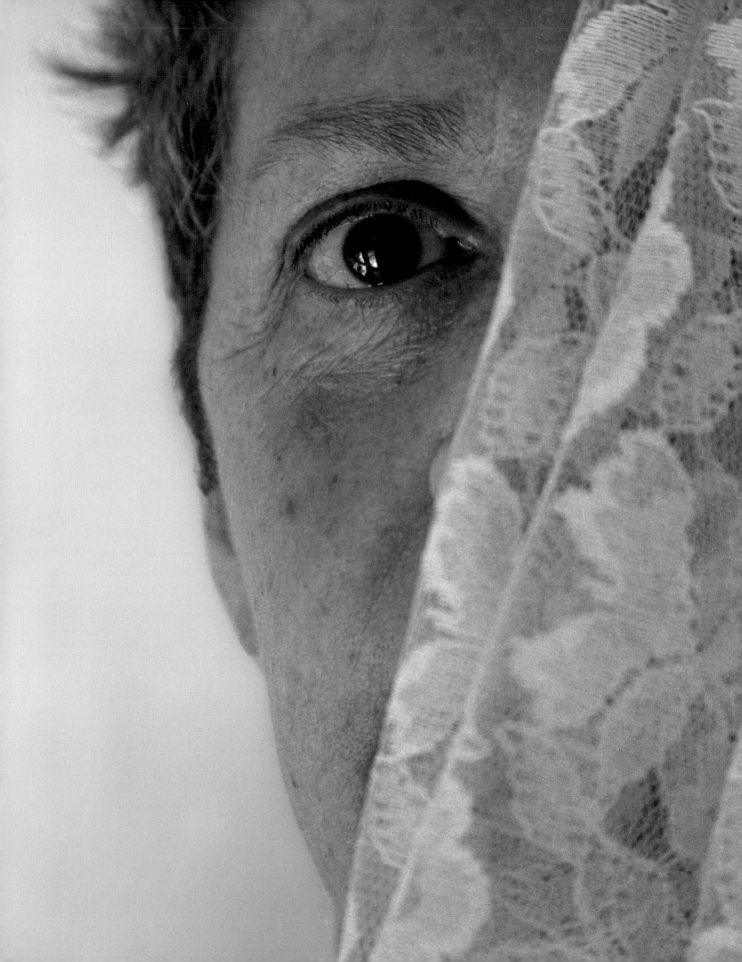

Sheila S.

"**M**y healing began in my eyes when I saw clearly for the first time. It was like that poem, 'through the glass darkly.' I was seeing through a fog or veil, and then it suddenly cleared. I saw that I had a choice. It was empowering to discover that I could get out of this situation."

Sheila was in an abusive marriage for four years before she was able to make that choice. Being Catholic, she feared excommunication from the church and the shame it would bring her parents if she ended the marriage.

"Every time he hit me, it was a total shock, like this wasn't really happening. My parents had never struck me; nobody had. He was very bright, had a Master's degree, and was an important person in his company, so it didn't make any sense to me. . . . But, he came from an alcoholic background; his father had abused his mother. I had no experience with this kind of thing and didn't know anyone who did, so I blamed myself and wondered what I was doing to make him hit me. I started drinking before he came home from work because the only way I could deal with him was with a couple of Manhattans under my belt.

"I had to get to the point where nothing mattered except escaping the situation. I was so sick and tired of being sick and tired that I just had to not care about the church or my parents shame. I was either going to kill myself or he was going to kill me."

Once she reached that moment of clarity, she left and never looked back.

"I had a good job as a social worker and was about to take a new job teaching at the local university, so I was able to take care of myself. I did what so many women in my situation can't seem to do, I reached out. I never hesitated to ask when I needed help. I had a very loving family and enormous support from friends.

"Once I made that decision to leave, it was life-changing. I've had two other life-changing events since: alcoholism and cancer. Each experience has changed my life and made me a better human being and so I try to be there for anyone else who is having problems in any of these areas. The message is that you come out better and more whole on the other side."

Post Interview Letter:

Theater is my profession and I've always believed it to be a powerful communicative force that should be much more than mere entertainment. When my good friend and photography teacher, Jan, shared her beginning ideas of what later would be the *Out of the Shadows* exhibit and the book *Women in Shadow and Light*, I knew that this kind of theater could be used somehow as a part of this project. As a survivor of domestic violence myself, I also had a very personal interest in doing it. When we decided to do the performance, I had lots of ideas about how to control it and do it and make it happen—and I'm glad none of them came to be. It just happened all on its own, and it touched me more than any other performance I've ever been associated with, proving to be the catalyst that cemented the original group forever. These incredible women, who weren't actors, got up and shared their strength and hope and their joy of surviving and supporting each other. This project was such an amazing coming together of so many elements that almost seemed to have a spiritual base to it, because things just flowed effortlessly. I was proud to be a part of it from the very beginning.

Photo by Brooke E. Schneider

Bobbie

"Doing something you love to do always helps you make it through. My work is an important part of my healing; it's very therapeutic. I love the way the clay caresses your skin. It's so physical, and you get a sense of release from it. When I combine it with music, it fills my emotional well to the point it bursts over. It's amazing what that can bring out in me."

Bobbie uses the things she loves to help her heal after two abusive marriages.

"I was so afraid of my first husband, I spent every moment of every day worrying what I might be doing wrong, what might set him off. My family's values made me feel I'd be damned to hell if I divorced, so it took a couple near-fatal attacks before I left. One where he had me by the throat, against a wall, feet off the floor, and I couldn't breathe. I never told anyone what was going on, because I was so ashamed. Once I started talking to someone, it helped me see it clearly. I woke up one day, and realized the spiritual divorce took place long ago, so signing a paper would be easy."

Divorcing a second time was even harder, but Bobbie was stronger.

"I was not being abused physically, so I thought, how bad can it be? But the emotional abuse was much worse, and I felt ashamed I'd let myself get into this again. I blamed myself. But this time I realized the key thing is to keep talking to people and not close yourself off. If there is something you are ashamed to talk about, that should be a big signal. You should be able to have total respect in the absence of total agreement with your partner. The lack of respect is what makes a relationship go wrong. It was a light bulb moment when I saw that in my marriage."

Each of these relationships has helped her to gain strength and wisdom.

"The universe gives us things that force us to grow, and I feel stronger than I ever have before. I know now that I do deserve respect, and my opinions and feelings are okay. I'm grateful that some of the painful things in my life can go on to help someone else."

Post-interview Letter:

Dear Jan,

It's so difficult to put language to the significance of being a part of this project. Abuse is an uncomfortable topic in our culture, where we prefer to see life in terms of fun and laughter. Abuse doesn't fit into that dialogue, so those of us who are being abused, or have been abused in the past, are encouraged to remain silent, seeing ourselves as shameful, even incompetent and worthless, because somehow we've "allowed" this event to "happen to us."

Speaking openly and publicly about the abuse has removed it from silence and shame, allowing others to help carry the load. Hopefully, it might also help someone else to avoid a similar situation.

This project has been a beam of the light shining into a very dark place.

Luoluo

"When I think of my healing journey, it's about finding my voice, and knowing my voice is worth hearing. It's getting in touch with my full range of emotions—including anger—and being able to speak up, to scream, to vocalize my feelings. Growing up, my role as a Chinese daughter was to be quiet and non-assertive, so I never developed my voice. The shame of the assault further stifled my voice, and I never really found it until my early thirties."

Luoluo was raped as a freshman in college by a sophomore she knew.

"He followed me home from a party, came into my residence hall and raped me. There wasn't awareness about acquaintance or date rape then, so I had no language to talk about what happened to me. I knew it was wrong, and it was physically and psychologically very painful. But I knew him, so I couldn't label it a rape. I tried to reach out and talk about it, and the counselor told me to stop rebelling against my parents with my sexuality. My boyfriend told me I was a slut. So I retreated inward, struggling for years, abusing myself and alcohol."

She felt she was damaged goods, not worthy of a good relationship.

"The rapist kept tracking me down throughout the next year and half and continued to coerce sex out of me; it was easy, because I had lost the ability to say 'no'—no longer believed I had the right to say 'no.' I tried to pretend that what happened was because he cared about me and wanted a relationship. He kept me believing I was ruined to have a relationship with anyone else. I had very long hair and he wrapped it around his neck, calling me Jezebel, creating a story about me enticing him. Later, when I began to understand what had happened to me and experience the anger, one of the first things I did was cut off my hair. I felt so free and powerful. I saw it as a symbolic lifting of the veil."

A turning point in healing was when a co-worker gave her a book to read.

"It was *They Never Called It Rape*. Once I had a name for it, and knew I hadn't done anything wrong, and that it happened to one in four other college women, I began to heal. It was also the beginning of my anger. I got involved in speaking and education on campus, and became very radical and feminist."

Still struggling with unresolved issues, Luoluo tried counseling again.

"She was supportive and validating, helping me to understand what happened, and to forgive myself. I was in grad school then, and I know the rape changed the path I was on. It made me want to be an educator, a social change agent. As dean of students at a major university, I can make decisions and changes, be an advocate. I am committed to bringing this and other social justice issues to the forefront. I know the man who raped me consumed Asian pornography and saw Asian women as passive victims, so I feel it was a racial assault as well as sexual. I am very sensitive to all these issues, both personally and in my job. When I was raped, I wrote to my dean and never even got a response. That experience colors the kind of dean I want to be.

"People at work see me as being a brick wall, impenetrable, and that scares me. Having been in a place of such vulnerability, I went way to the other extreme as I healed, being super strong. I thought I had to fight my way back by never being vulnerable again, but it's not true. I want to be both vulnerable *and* strong, and one way I can do that is by learning to laugh and be playful again. My name in Chinese means happiness, and reconnecting with my name is an important part of healing. I own all parts of me now. I am human, I am whole, and I have a strong clear voice."

Marisa

"I love this photograph of me, and I like it that the scar through my eyebrow is just barely included in the picture. When you were photographing me, I remember turning my face to the sun. It felt good, as if the sun could heal the scar, and heal me."

At age twenty-one, this scar marked the end of a volatile relationship with her first real love.

"He was very passionate—but also extremely volatile, jealous and possessive. Any sign of me trying to be independent made him crazy. I should have seen the red flags when he was verbally abusive and shoved me around, but I was so in love I missed it. When he gave me this scar, he was hitting me in the face with his fist so hard that it knocked me down and my head hit the corner of a cabinet. He took me to the hospital for stitches, and he was so apologetic and swore it'd never happen again. But I knew I had to leave him. Now the scar is a daily reminder to me."

Marisa grew up in an abusive family, and was determined to break the cycle of abuse. She had studied art in Milwaukee, and decided to go to Italy to continue her work.

"I just wanted to be as far away as I could, so my mom helped me to get to Italy. It was the best thing I could've done for myself. Otherwise I know that I would've been tempted to go back to him. I saw Mom being abused my whole childhood, and I had to do everything I could to get myself out of that situation. My mom stayed with my step-dad thirteen years—'for the kids'—and it was horrible, hearing the fights and seeing him beat her. My son will never see a man hit me."

Her mother escaped the abuse by leaving with another man when Marisa was sixteen.

"I was happy for her at first, but I have some anger about it because he abused us more when she left. So we ran away and got in trouble and did drugs. My mom was verbally abusive and she had been abused by her mother, too. It's a cycle that will keep repeating unless someone breaks it. I am going to be the one to stop that cycle.

"I've been through lots of therapy, worked hard to feel good about myself and get my self-esteem back. I still have some insecurities, but I know I'm a good mom and a good artist. I think that being able to do something creative really helped me heal. I'm so grateful to have my art and dance because it gives me a good sense of self-worth."

Laura D.

"The piano is the first hobby I've pursued in my adult life. One of the ways I responded to being abused was believing my value was only in what I could produce and do; so I focused on that to the exclusion of other things in my life. Coming back to the piano is one way I am reclaiming my right to 'be,' to enjoy life in the moment, and not have to prove that I have a right to exist through what I do. It's been many years since I was a victim, and I'm not just an incest survivor anymore. I'm a human being trying to find my way back to wholeness."

Her grandfather sexually abused Laura from about age three, but she was able to suppress those memories until she was twenty-seven.

"It always happened around him putting me to bed and telling me a story. He was a very Orthodox Jewish man, and we'd go up for the Sabbath, arriving before the start of Shabbat, Friday at sundown. They weren't allowed to turn lights on or off on those days, so there was one little light that was on all the time. That's what I'd focus on; I'd disappear into that light.

"When I was in my first committed relationship, and sex and intimacy got connected, I wasn't able to be sexual. The pressure for sex from my partner brought the first memory. It was a moment of deep truth; knowledge that had always been there broke free. I could deny it and not want it to have happened, but in that moment I knew it was true."

Once she realized she'd been abused, Laura turned to her mother.

"There was a wonderful side of my family life; a lot of attention to intellectual development and creativity, being socially and politically active, and doing a lot together. But my mother saw me as an extension of her, so it created tension in our relationship. My revealing the sexual abuse was the last in a long line of conflicts about me not being the daughter she wanted. She was supportive at first but then she realized what it meant for her; she was torn between her daughter and her father, even though he was dead already. It was devastating for both of us.

"I felt so raw and vulnerable and undone, and expected support from her. She was furious and didn't believe it had happened. For years, I was angry and hated her and didn't want anything to do with her. I felt abandoned and alone."

Six months after her first memories, Laura approached Ellen Bass about co-writing a book that would eventually become The Courage to Heal.

"Ellen had already written a book, and knew how much work it was, so she said no. I was single, obsessed with sexual abuse, and had a desperate need to express something. I said I would do all the interviewing the first year, and she finally agreed.

"I cried through every interview as if they were talking about *my* life. I was in the emergency stage and I used those interviews as a lifeline, since the women I was interviewing were so much farther along than I was. During this time, I had no relationship with my mother, and when the book came out, she and all her relatives were infuriated. From their point of view, I was not only telling lies about her father; I was doing it on national TV. It was all I talked about. I'd meet someone and say, 'Hi, I'm Laura Davis and I'm an incest survivor.' I looked at everything through the lens of abuse."

Writing and living the book was also a major part of Laura's healing.

"I saw a therapist every week for six years, I joined incest groups, I read everything I could. But all the books said if you were sexually abused, your life was ruined. The theory we put forth started to work in my life; you have to believe it happened, make a conscious decision to heal, and know it is not an intellectual process. Just face it and feel it and talk about it, and know it *is* possible to heal. I had to surrender to healing, and writing was a big part of it. Finally I got to the point that sexual abuse was not the center of my life."

Laura's reaction to the incredible success of the book was unexpected

"I feel I was meant to do it and in some ways like I fulfilled my purpose when it came out. But it was also uncomfortable. People saw me as an icon, not a real person. I was invisible, and that was how I felt when I was being abused. I wasn't spiritually grounded then, and I didn't know how to listen to people without absorbing their pain."

She spent five years on the road doing talks and workshops on her best-selling book. Then external pressures combined with her own needs to make her pull back.

"My work was keeping me in the experience of incest, and my healing had progressed to a point where I didn't need that anymore. I just wanted to be a human being. I also met my partner, Karyn, at that time. I helped raise her son, and had two more children with her in the next five years. My family was happy I wasn't out waving the flag anymore, and the grandchildren provided the impetus for my mother and I to try and reconnect.

"My mother first found out I was a lesbian when I was twenty-three and said I'd confirmed her worst fears. But by the time the abuse thing came out she had totally accepted that I was gay and that gave me hope we could work out the incest issue as well. Over years of trying and many disasters, we got to the point of agreeing to disagree. I knew I was not going to change her mind, but I had healed enough I didn't *need* her to believe me anymore; I knew the incest had happened and that was enough. Being a parent, I was more compassionate to my mother as a parent, and knew she did the best she could. We both had a very strong intention to reconcile, and that is a powerful thing. Of anything I've done in my life, I feel proudest of the fact that we are close after not speaking for years, and she says the same.

"To reconcile meant having a broader perspective, like an aerial view. I understand generations of trauma, and my mom's childhood with the man who abused me. It's less about me as a victim or him as a perpetrator, and it seems so much more human now, and less sinister. These are the factors that made me the person I am, and I don't have the kind of anger or outrage I had before. I just accept it. The sexual abuse was one of many factors that shaped me, and I don't identify myself by how I was wounded.

"The most profound part of the healing process began long after I relinquished my identification with being a survivor of abuse. My history remained unchanged, but the way I related to it underwent a dramatic transformation. I chose to be a human being who was struggling to grow, rather than someone whose life was determined by something that had happened to me as a child.

"Now I'm dealing with the abuse on a more spiritual level. A baby comes into the world with trust, connection, belief they belong and deserve to be taken care of. When I was abused all that was severed, so I'm reclaiming that innocence, I'm learning how to trust and to be vulnerable and surrender. I never wanted to be vulnerable; I'm a strong survivor. Now I'm going to a place of surrender to find out who I am behind the strong powerful woman. I'm giving up the control I've had to exert in every aspect of my life.

"In the *Courage to Heal,* we said the backbone of healing is anger, but now I don't really believe that. Anger is a great motivator in the early stages; it makes us stand up for ourselves and speak out and cut ties with people who are hurting us, and choose life when suicide seems easier. Now I would say connection is the heart of healing; how do we get reconnected? That's the continuing journey. I feel like there's a transformative process happening in me that I couldn't stop if I wanted to. I'm trying to let go and let it happen instead of making things happen as I always have. I'm much more in the present moment than I ever have been."

Carla & Samantha

Flossie

"Well, I get along pretty good, and I don't make a big deal out of nothing. Here I am, I'm ninety-four, and I've got my family and a nice place to live. I have never regretted leaving."

Flossie left her forty-year marriage when she was sixty-two. For her generation, abuse seemed to be an accepted way of life, and it took extraordinary strength to leave.

"I guess I was a pretty brave woman to leave at that age. Under the influence he'd get a little rough and hit me—not severely—but enough to say it was wrong. And he hit the boys, too. One day I came home and there had been an argument, and he wanted me to tell the two boys to get out of my home. I said, 'I wouldn't give them up for the king, why should I give them up for you?' I packed my bag and went to my daughter's, and that was it. I didn't go back."

Many of Flossie's eight children are in abusive relationships, including the father of her granddaughter, Carla. This cycle of abuse passed to Carla, and if it is not broken, it will continue, ad infinitum. *Flossie's support enabled Carla to break that cycle in her family. Carla was present at Flossie's interview, and adds this:*

"Grandma's children didn't have the tools to break the cycle of abusive behavior stemming from this one man. The effects will continue in every generation unless we stand up and say *'No more!'* We have to step out of the shadows, take control and end the cycle.

"Grandma never has a bad word to say about anybody, and she taught me about unconditional love. She was my support when I was trying to leave my abusive marriage. I'm so glad she can be a part of this project, and help me to stop this cycle in our family."

One year later, Carla is by Flossie's side as she struggles to recover from a stroke.

"Today I sit with her in the hospital, knowing it may be the last time I see this remarkable woman. As I leave, she tells me I am beautiful and she loves me. I tell her how beautiful she is inside and out, and that she is strong and in control. She smiled that Flossie-smile and raised her arm up in a sign of victory."

Annee

"Healing to me is having my legs, my feet, and not being paralyzed anymore. If I get dissociated or too wound up, I pound my feet and walk really strong on the ground and I'll come back. I need to be grounded. When your feet are touching Mother Earth, you're standing on everything that ever was."

When Annee was thirty-one, she quit using alcohol and drugs, and at the urging of friends, went to a women's treatment center in Half Moon Bay.

"At the center everyone was given a book to read, and I got *Betrayal of Innocence*. It had case studies of incest, and the mother-son study sounded exactly like my grandmother and father. It was uncanny how similar the man was to my father; never cheated on his wife, church every Sunday, kind of hyper-responsible and hyper-moral. The next evening something almost hypnotic drew me back to the book. I opened it and realized that although I'd read it twice, I had somehow skipped the section on father-daughter incest. When I read it, I went into convulsions and was paralyzed from the waist down. I was screaming, freaking out, and I didn't know why, because it never, ever, ever occurred to me this could happen. My father was the moral holder of our family. If anyone had a problem, they went to him. In that one minute my life just blew up. It was two hours before I could walk again. Now I think the paralysis related to the fact I was raped below the waist, and it's probably also why it is so important to me to be grounded."

Though she had been a psychiatric nurse for years, nobody ever talked about incest. Although she would go through many years of therapy, she was able to begin her healing immediately in that supportive environment.

"One of the most gracious things was this happened after I got sober, and I was in a recovering community. I stayed in that remote place and didn't get my car or my things or talk to my parents for two years. I was dissociating and so out of control in the beginning, but therapy and amazing non-traditional healers helped me move through stuff without an immense amount of shame. One of the most powerful things was model mugging, which I advise every survivor to do. It is a self-defense empowerment program for women, and you get to act out what happened to you, and fight until you win this time."

She had sodium amatol interviews to help fill in the blanks. When she finally told her parents on the phone, her father denied it and got very angry.

"If they had given me one crumb of support I would've spent years trying to take care of them, and re-pressed everything, so I guess it was for the best. I needed to be on my own."

Her father went into the hospital shortly afterwards with cardiomyopathy and slowly died over the next six years. She moved to Mexico and only saw him once in that time, when her brother called to say their father was dying.

"I was so much like my dad, so it's sad. He taught me how to draw, and use a camera, and garden; all the things I love. When I saw him in the hospital, he was emaciated and weak, and said he'd lost control of his body. I looked him in the eye and said, 'I relate.' It was the longest minute, and then we were both sobbing. He denied it, but then said let's put it all behind us. It was dramatic and intense. He was a man who couldn't face his stuff and let it eat his heart out."

Annee's trauma has become a healing gift for others.

"A few years after this came up, I had a job in a psych hospital for women and we began treating dissociative disorders. I was so afraid I'd be fired if they knew my history, but decided to come out to my boss about it. She said, 'Thank God you're here; none of us know what to do.' That's where the big healing came for me. This thing that was so shameful to me became such a valuable gift, not only to those who were wounded, but also to the people who were helping them. Now that is my life. I am still a nurse, and I give talks all over the world that help empower women."

"Yes, the experience was traumatic and awful, but it also changed my life in so many positive ways that I can't really say I wish it hadn't happened. It allowed me to develop a degree of compassion, empathy and caring that I never would have otherwise. I have much to be grateful for."

Carmen

"When I think of healing, I think of my hands, because I always used them to protect my face when he beat me. And when I was raped, I made a fist when the guy was on top of me, and tried to hold him away from me. Now I can use my hands for good things."

Carmen was drawn into an abusive relationship at nineteen, and felt unable to escape when she became pregnant.

"I see now that he was very controlling even before the abuse, doing things like buying me expensive gifts, so I'd be dependent on him. The first time he hit me, I was driving, and he hit me with his fist, in the head. I was so shocked I didn't know what to do. I enrolled in college in another city, hoping that would be the end of it. But then I discovered I was pregnant, so I had to move back in with my parents—who were always very supportive and loving. They never saw the abuse and I was ashamed to tell them. I felt trapped because now I really was financially dependent on him, with no school, no job and a son to raise."

When her son was one-and-a-half, she went out to buy diapers late one night and was carjacked, kidnaped and raped.

"That assault saved me. The night of the rape, I told Mom the rapist held a gun to me and I wished he had shot me, so I could just die and not have to deal with this for the rest of my life. I felt like death walking in a body. But I went to counseling immediately after the assault, and put all my energy into healing. I wanted to heal, and knew I couldn't do it with him, so the trauma became a catalyst. The assault strengthened me, and made me see things differently. I saw it as a way to escape my violent relationship. Because of that assault, I became a powerful person, an advocate."

She completed a degree in police science, planning to pursue a law enforcement career, but then decided she could better serve in other areas.

"I got a degree in criminology and law studies and began work at a sexual assault center. Now I work with the Task Force on Family Violence, and helped form a support group for domestic violence and sexual assault, because they so often go together. I'm doing good work, and I'm married to a sweet, sensitive man. People were so surprised when they knew I was in an abusive relationship; they always saw me as such a strong person. It was easy to help friends, but I'm glad I finally took my own advice. I'm in a very good place now."

Kathy

"For me, the most important thing in healing is my meditation practice. Meditation and therapy is how I feel I'm going to get through this. Journaling helps me too, because I lose the thinking mind and just write. Things come out that surprise me."

Kathy was sexually abused twice; from about age three to age five, and then from about age eight to twelve. Both times it was by hired hands living on the family farm.

"The second one I remember more because I was older I think; it was a game, our little secret. I was a tomboy, and I would ride on the tractor or meet him in the barn, and he would give me candy or take me out for a cone. I think I knew it was wrong, but it was not painful or forced, so I didn't think it affected me. At twelve, I said it had to stop, and then when I was in high school, I tried to tell my boyfriend about it and he freaked out. So I never told anyone else until I was in a women's studies class my last year in college. But I still didn't feel like it had affected my life. It happened and I had moved on . . . . Right."

During a recent breath work session, when she was looking for answers about relationship issues, she saw how much it really has affected her.

"It came screaming out; I sobbed for three hours. I've spent the last several years trying to find out who I am and develop my spirituality, and knew there was something blocking. In the breath work, I was trying to understand the difficulties I've had with relationships; always being with men ten or fifteen years older than me, that I know are wrong for me, but not being able to say no and walk away. Now I saw it was all about those childhood incidences, and knowing it was wrong, but not being able to say no. The pattern started when I was eight. I realized the anger was as much at me as at him, because I knew it was wrong, but I couldn't stop it. I was not able to be in control then so I've decided to never be vulnerable, always be in control by being in relationships I knew I would leave. That's what I'm dealing with now."

She is slowly breaking through that wall she built around herself..

"It was so buried, I had to drop to the depths of pain to realize I needed to do something. At times I'd like to crawl back to the unawareness hole; but in reality, I wasn't even alive, I didn't feel. These tears are new to me; I never cried before, and I know some of them concern grieving about never being a kid. A big part of who I am is because of this experience. Some of it I appreciate, like my independent spirit. My goal is to find the areas in my life that are problematic, that I think relate back to these incidents, and realize I don't have to react to them the way I always have. At this point, my life is committed to continuing to process and becoming more fully alive."

sitting quietly I wait
patiently—not a peep, not a twitch
to see if today is the day the doors will open
what's that I see—a crack widening
a soft pink sweetness seeps out
a childlike innocence glides thru the door
startled, I shift—seeing me then she slides
back thru the door, but not before
it slams
shut
breaking off
a little bit of her
which falls to the earth
withering, the life seeps out of
this piece of her
turning brown and shriveling
she's lost in the humus of the forest floor

and again I sit—determined
this time to wait until those doors open
again, allowing me a glimpse of her
patience awarded—a slit of light
but no not this!—a black slime
oozes across the floor
a darkness, long buried,
forgotten—no desire to bring it back—
it comes roaring out of those doors—no—
no, this is not she, the she I'm looking for

barricade the doors—force it back
slamming shut—but not before some
of the ooze drips down onto her
now decaying body part
I turn my back—no more
I can't risk it—I'll stay where I am
go back from where I've come
when I feel a tickle on my heel
climbing up my calf
growing around and up my legs
a soft green tendril, a sprout
a new life emerging out of what had died
a new she growing enriched by the muck

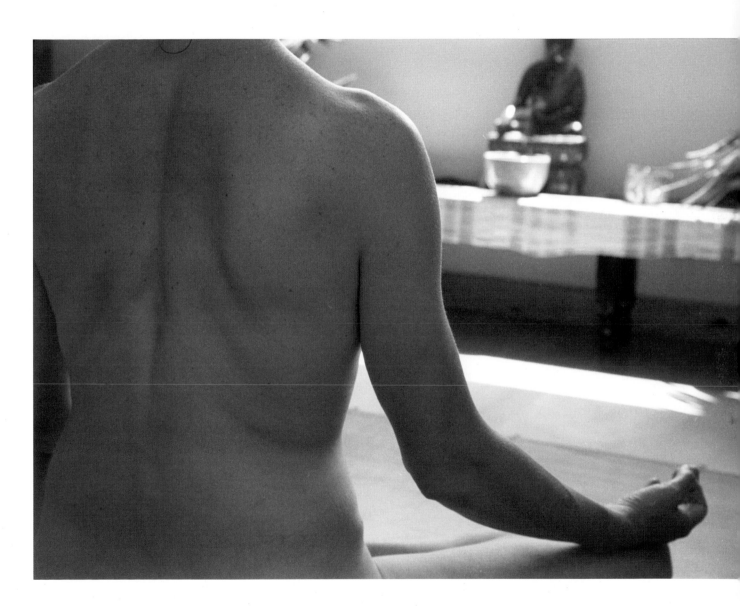

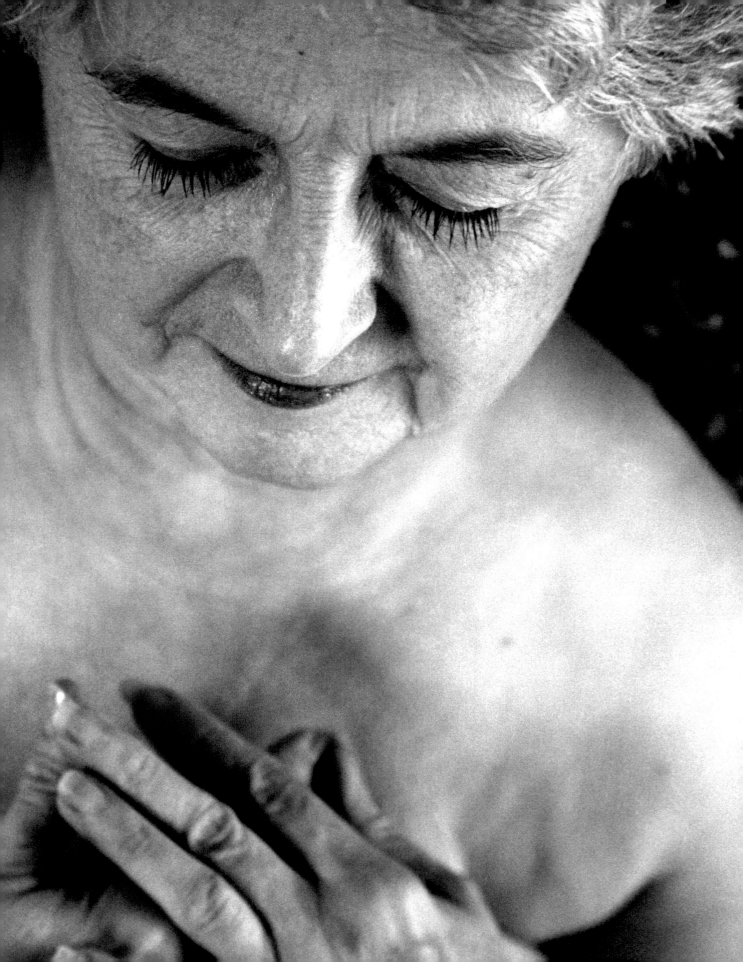

Bonnie

"For the most part, I feel at peace now, in my heart. Although this experience destroyed my faith in organized religion, my spirituality is still alive in my heart, and that is healing. Even the church could not destroy that."

Bonnie was married twenty-four years to a minister who became very abusive.

"He was charismatic and charming, but soon after we married little things started happening that made me feel unsafe and less of a person. First there were mind games, then he began throwing things at me, pushing me around, and calling me horrible names like 'Old Shitface.'

"I went to the doctor with severe chest pains, sure I was having a heart attack. I couldn't breathe. They couldn't find anything physically wrong and sent me to a psychiatrist. This confirmed what my husband had been telling me—I was crazy and if I got my head straightened out, we'd have a good marriage. I bought it because I loved this man."

She kept trying to make it better, but the harder she tried, the worse it got, and the more depressed she became. She went to a bishop in the church for help, saying she wanted to go to a women's shelter. He warned her against it, and it was another five years before she dared seek help again.

"Every week, he'd stand up in front of the church and act like Mr. Wonderful, so nobody could believe he would do anything wrong. They all thought it was my problem. So when I went back to the bishop, the church sent my husband to treatment for his anger issues, and I spent two months in a psychiatric hospital. I went back, and it was better for awhile. But one night my son, who was recovering from a serious car accident and barely able to walk, had to step between us to protect me. It was then I knew someone could die if I didn't leave."

A friend referred her to a shelter where they had a group for older battered women.

"In the group, I finally realized that this was abuse just as much as having broken bones. And it was escalating so much, I know if I'd stayed, I'd have broken bones by now. From that group I got involved with the Coalition Against Domestic Violence, and the work I did with them helped me to heal. I've also been doing some work at a medical school, helping doctors to pick up on verbal and psychological abuse so they can help women get to a shelter or talk to someone before they get physically hurt. This offers hope.

"At the end of the day, I look back to see if there is anything I've done that's made a difference in someone's life. I feel good about what I am doing, and that is empowering."

Kim

"What helps me heal is trying to think back to what I liked to do as a young girl of thirteen or fourteen; what made me happy then, before the whole confusion of relationships. Just getting away from the complicated feeling of being an adult. I think of things like being in the garden with my mom, riding bikes, walking in the woods, playing in the trees, going to the beach. What made me happy then still makes me happy now, sure enough. So I try to do things like that more. I try to get back to when I started becoming who I am, and maybe I can change the path and make a new life."

What wisdom there is in Kim's words; finding the child she lost. She is discovering her voice again after ending a violent relationship. When she left, she had no voice after he strangled her repeatedly. Like many women, she felt the emotional and mental abuse hurt her even more than the brutal physical beatings.

"He told me a big sob story, and being a nurturing person, I wanted to take care of him and make it all go away. But of course, I couldn't help him or change him, and it just got worse. I learned you have to take care of yourself first. I was beaten down so much emotionally, I didn't think anyone else would ever have me. The emotional part was the worst of it. My friends have been wonderful. They are helping me get my self-esteem back, and to see that it wasn't my fault. I can call them any time, and if they see me starting to get depressed again, they put me back together."

One of the catalysts for Kim to leave was her children. Now she sees them as part of her inspiration to create a new and better life.

"I just want to get back to being the independent person I was and taking care of myself and my children. If I'm better, they'll be better. I'm going back and creating a new beginning. It really helps me being creative in my work, creating beautiful things and using my mind for something other than negatives.

"I think about every move I make, and I'm so conscious of the way I relate to my children. I don't want that to ever come back again, in my life, or my children's lives. Just talking about it is good, because sometimes you just don't see how terribly wrong it is for anyone to treat a human being that way until you tell someone about it.

"I'm relearning how to have a relationship, starting with myself. Just loving myself is a new thing."

Post Interview Letter:

I would like to thank you for including me in this amazingly enriching project. My involvement with you and the other women who are participating helped me grow and heal in ways that are difficult to put into words. It strengthens me knowing that my story can help other people who may feel there is no way out. There always is.

Kim

Emily

"**M**y hands really helped me heal. Being in bodywork helped eliminate the shame and guilt that there was something wrong with me. The most healing thing was having the memories come out; in my heart. It was just 'ahhh' (a big sigh)!"

Memories of infant sexual abuse by her father shed new light on old feelings.

"Most of my life I didn't like my dad, but I didn't know why. And I used to be afraid of all men. When it came out it, I was like 'wow, it all makes sense now.' I talked with my dad and he was crying and saying how sorry he was, and I was crying. Once it was out, the forgiveness was already there."

Her three sisters were also sexually abused. To heal, they've all done family and individual therapy, including their father.

"Had I not had therapy, I don't think I'd be alive. I took it as if I had done something wrong, I'm not worthy, and I hated myself. Now I realize it's not who I am, it's just something that happened to me. I did therapy so I wouldn't pass this on to my son. I found out both my parents were abused as children, and I wanted to break the cycle. My attitude now is to have gratitude for what you have, and compassion for yourself and for the person who initiated the abuse.

"My dad doesn't remember what he did to us because he drank so much then. It must have been horrible for him to live with it. He is a very different person now, and he has always been there for us. He has been like a father to my son, as well as a grandpa.

"I think if you've never been abused, it's easy to imagine it doesn't happen much, and I have learned a lot from this. It's not an awful secret, and you should talk about it. Often by talking about it, you can help someone else. People have incredible adversity in their lives, and do amazing things in spite of it, even because of it. When life is tough, it always helps me to help somebody else. I just want to do my work and continue making a difference with my life."

Barb

"It's been very hard for me to give to myself in any way, because for so long I've felt I'm not worthy. Even little luxuries like time for myself, or a hot bath are things I crave, but have a hard time giving myself. I'm really good at taking care of everyone else before myself. I was beautiful once, and felt worthy and confident, before all the ugliness."

Barb was seventeen and a virgin when she felt that beauty. Her boyfriend was a year older and in the military. On a visit home he raped her.

"I fought hard and scratched his back badly. He was so proud of those scratches and bragged to his buddies. I was in denial after it happened, even after I found out I had gotten pregnant from that assault. After six months, my mom figured it out, and then the shame of being pregnant became even worse than the shame of the assault."

She had to leave school before graduation, when her mother insisted on keeping the pregnancy a secret.

"My mother wanted the child adopted, and my dad said no, so there was conflict in the family. I remember thoughts of suicide. But once I felt the child move, I decided I still wanted to live. I realized it was not the child's fault, and it deserved to live, too, no matter how it began. I was so torn about what to do, so I placed him in foster care. I went away to college for a semester, and then I came back and brought home this baby who did not know me."

Barb later rekindled a relationship with an old boyfriend. After they married, he adopted her son. Still, she waited sixteen years to tell him, and their children, about the rape.

"I tried to tell my husband a couple times about the assault, but just could not do it. Finally, I had to tell him why I was feeling so bad and having nightmares again when my son joined the army. He got a buzz haircut, and he looked so much like his biological father, it was like seeing a ghost. My two daughters know of the assault, too. My oldest daughter was raped at fourteen, and I learned that this often happens, that assault can follow through generations. I wanted to help her move forward, and through her counseling I got a lot of healing for myself. She made a police report and got an arrest and conviction. That helped us all as a family.

"The only other time I've ever talked about my rape before this, it was a disaster. I had objectified it so much; I was afraid to be vulnerable, and I didn't know how to say 'this happened to me.' That was eight years ago. Being part of this project, the focus was always on healing, which is what made it possible for me to come out of hiding. I hope this can help others as well. I know there are many like me who've locked away a similar incident. I hope when people read this, they won't say, 'Oh my God, how awful,' but just say, 'Thank you for sharing your story.' This process has been wonderful, being able to let go of the ugliness in me. I think the beauty was there in me all along, but denying it was part of the wall I built. Maybe this will help me feel beautiful again."

Post Interview Letter:

Jan,

How has *Out of the Shadows / Women in Shadow and Light* affected me?

I am not afraid of the secret anymore. How I would wonder, does that person know? Am I marked and can people see that mark? Always very cautious, always afraid someone would confront me or challenge me. There have been times I wanted to shout from the roof, "I know this hurt." But something inside said, they wouldn't believe you, it will only cause pain. Focusing on the healing has helped me the most. You did not judge, you did not push for details of the event, you accepted me as I was and what I had to offer. Yes, I am a survivor; yes I have been on this healing journey all along. I just did not recognize it.

I *was* the peacemaker all my life, the one who counseled. It seemed when I stopped doing that all hell broke loose. I have to remind myself that I am not responsible for anyone else's actions or behaviors. That new confidence you talked about? I am looking out for me. Perhaps that sounds selfish, but I now have strength, and I now remind myself to take care of me first so that there is something left to share with others. I am a happier person; I am enjoying my life and my partner.

The words from Jeanie's song *Riverbed*—"this time I'm fighting for me," says it. *For Me.* This project has given me permission to look at me. (I take bubble baths every chance I can now.) I look at what I need and deserve as a survivor— as a woman. Meeting the other participants, sharing in creating the segments for the performance. Together we shared pain, encouragement and anger. I was really surprised by the anger, that *I* still had anger and that I was not alone. Together as a group we went public.

This project was very empowering. I thought I had all the counseling I needed, but this was different, it moved me beyond the healing process. This time I *am* fighting for me. . . I did this project for me; this is *my* story. It is about a different kind of assertiveness—a different kind of confidence. I am not sure that I can explain it; I feel it inside. Yes, I was very frightened to go public, very much afraid of what people would think. What my parents and siblings might say; would they disown me, tell me I've really lost it? My partner and adult children were very supportive. There was such a huge outpouring of love and support from people I knew and people that I just met. I felt extremely comfortable and very much supported. A few people have come up to me since and said, "I, too, know your hurt. I was abused, too."

If it helps just one person. . . .

Barb

I Don't Want to Fight Any More....

Once I was young and beautiful,
full of life, light and energy

Then I was darkness and silent.

I fought when you hurt me,
My soul cried out.

I fought with my hands.
You laughed and showed off the marks.

I fought the shame and the ugliness.
You haunted my dreams.
I fought with denial, not wanting to remember,
not wanting to feel again.

I fought to keep you hidden in my soul.
I fought to forget you

But you kept returning.

My soul has been set free.
I have found peace, security, and love.

No more will I fight
No more will I hide.

I have spread my wings
I fly.

Jeanne V.

"When I left, those bricks on my shoulders just fell off. I could breathe, and I didn't feel tired or tight anymore. I can't raise my arms much because I have such bad arthritis, but I felt like a bird or a butterfly . . . I felt like I could fly!"

Jeanne was in her sixties when she finally took flight. With the support of HELP and the local sheriff, she packed her things and left a marriage of forty-three years. Those years as a farm wife were not only filled with hard physical labor, but also with verbal, emotional and sexual abuse.

"I was in denial for so many years, and I never felt good about myself until the day I moved out. Then I said, 'I did it, and I'm not going back no matter where I end up.' I was flying like a bird, I was *free!*"

Jeanne couldn't be happier with her decision, and has learned so much from her experience that she wants to pass on to other women.

"I urge girls in that situation to please . . . look at yourself and what you want out of life. Realize if you're in an abusive situation it is not going to get better, and you can't ever change the other person. For women of my generation, there wasn't much help. People didn't really talk about it; it was just the way it was and you sometimes lived in a hell you just had to put up with. Now there is so much more support available. You have to talk to someone, even if it's an anonymous phone help line. Whatever you do, don't keep it all bottled inside.

"I talked to a counselor years ago who told me the only thing I can change is myself, and I didn't pay attention. It took me way too long, but I did it, and now I can breathe. I am free, and I have my life back. It's never too late to be happy."

Compassion

"I converted to Islam in 1993 and that was a great part of my healing. It helped me get grounded and find peace. If I held onto the anger I couldn't have moved. So I opened my hands, let go of the anger, and picked up things that were valuable to me. I did volunteer work, got involved with causes, and went through a lot of transformation."

That change came after she escaped a fifteen-year abusive relationship.

"I didn't know what abuse was, had never been exposed to it. At first it was verbal, but about ten years into it, it escalated to physical abuse as well. My children were grown, it was just he and I, and I knew it was unsafe. But he knew how to hide it, so the few people I confided in didn't believe it. And he'd send flowers to work, so they all thought he was great. I got to really despise him. It wasn't healthy for me to live like that, not only for the abuse, but that I despised him so. I was beginning to hate him to the point where, maybe he run in front of a car and it'll kill him. I was looking for options to get out, but didn't know how. I was scared. Then one evening he attempted to kill me."

She was afraid to go to her family, so she went to a shelter.

"He would have hung around my family, trying to find me. I took a leave of absence, and stayed in the shelter until I could get it together. With the help of people from the shelter, I had the locks changed, and secured my belongings, so he had to move out of the apartment. After he couldn't find me, and nobody would help him, he went back to Chicago."

Three years later, illness made it impossible for her to work. Then her oldest son passed away, and she found herself again trying to hold on with both hands.

"I had to let go of any anger or animosity, or it would have smothered me. You don't hold on to trash. If I held on, other things would pile on top of that. I think that's where a lot of women end up, continually being a victim. You never know when the healing comes because you're so busy feeling sorry."

Healing allowed her to let her guard down and open up to life. Last year she got married, in an arranged marriage, since her religion does not allow dating.

"He's gentle and understanding, and I can be myself. I'm happy and at peace. You're only a victim as long as you want to be, and I couldn't see myself holding onto saying I'm a victim forever. And I don't call myself a survivor because that's another handle. It's all part of the journey and we never know where life is going to take us. As one door closed another opened. That's what the journey is about. You learn from it."

Miriam

"I'm ready to spend some time alone, and some time with God. I need time I can really call my own, to pray and to figure out where I need to go next in my life. It helps me to just walk in the woods or on the beach, to have that quiet time just to be with myself."

Miriam left her abusive marriage when her husband also began to abuse their teenage daughter.

"The abuse started the first week we were married. He would throw me across a room or into a wall. When I would try to talk to him about it later, he would ask what I was talking about. He goes into a rage and attacks me, and seems not to realize he did it. He kind of dissociates. Like many women, I thought I could put up with it, but when it gets laid on our daughters, it's not okay. He threw my daughter against the couch, and then went in and grabbed two guns, and said, "What am I going to have to do to control this family?" I told the police and got a restraining order against him. As hard as it was, I did my children a favor by leaving and saying this is not okay behavior."

The difficulty of leaving was compounded by her family being very prominent in the community, and by the fact that she and her husband were an integral part of the family business.

"I didn't want people to think badly of my family; we owned a big business and I didn't want it to affect that. I didn't want my dad to lose trust in us, since my husband and I were running the business together."

Once she finally left, she realized she had been taking care of everyone but herself.

"I wanted my parents to be happy, so I worked hard to make sure they were okay. I did the same in my marriage. I felt responsible for everyone. I thought I was strong and could help him, but he just wanted me to join him in his insanity. I would have helped him more if I had just left a long time ago. I finally realize I can be happy even if he isn't."

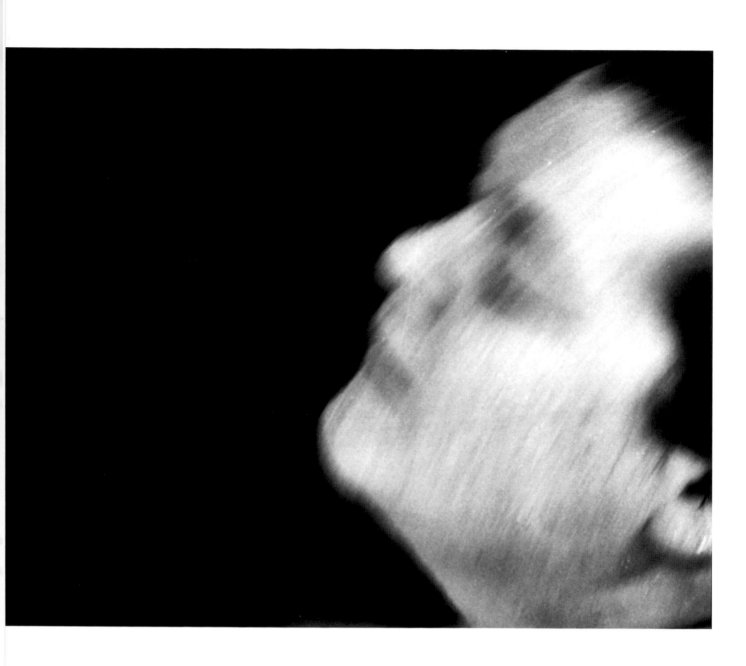

Milli

"The shower was my first sense of relief and release. I spent three hours in there and worked a lot of stuff out in that first shower. I felt my mind healing; I was in the shower and realized the voices were gone. I finally washed them out, so healing could begin."

Milli was five when her father first sexually abused her.

"He raped me, and I was bleeding for days. But he wouldn't take me to the hospital. The abuse lasted until I was eight, and then he disappeared. He always told me this is how daddies love their little girls, and it was our secret. So I never told my mom.

"I was also sexually abused later by my older brother, and physically abused by a younger brother."

At sixteen, Milli had a breakdown and attempted suicide.

"My mom put me in a hospital and I was there eight months. I was diagnosed as manic-depressive, but I later learned I had developed multiple personalities to cope with the abuse."

At twenty-two, she had another breakdown after three men raped her.

"I grew up thinking the way you get love and acceptance from men was to have sex, so I slept around. When I was raped I thought somehow I deserved it because of my slutty behavior, so I never told anyone. I had struggled for years to get my life back, and those men took so much from me. After that I just went through the motions of living. I was tired of always hurting, and always being a victim.

"I finally found a therapist I could trust and he suggested keeping a journal as a way to deal with the multiple personalities. That helped me in the process of integrating into a whole person."

Meditation and affirmations have also helped her to heal.

"I do the affirmations every day to remind myself I'm a good person. I realize now I was using food for everything, whether it was celebration, sorrow or anger. I was almost four hundred pounds. Now I have more confidence, I'm losing weight and feeling better about myself.

"This project is helping me to trust again. Trusting another person with my story and seeing that they won't use it against me is a huge leap for me. I'm thankful to all the courageous women who are part of this project. Their courage showed me that I too can heal, and be a strong woman. I feel like this will help me as well as others."

Post Interview Letter:

Hi Jan,

It did me so much good to redo the photo. It was surprising how it helped me put things in a different perspective. My new motto is "do over" . . . meaning if it doesn't work one way, then do it over another way. I have really grown a lot since meeting you.

The interview and photo played a big part in my new growth. The interview was the first time I put any distance between me and my history. I was finally able to get past a lot of emotional baggage and truly examine the events for what they were . . . acts of control, final outcomes of eternal battles, the results of previous abuse. I wasn't the only victim . . . so were my brother and my father. As much as it cost me, it cost them, too. I'm not sure if they even knew it or not, but I know it in my soul. Realizing all that took me to the ultimate place for survivors, as my new philosophy shows: real inner peace. All I have to do when something isn't the way I like it is . . . do it all over again. Start fresh. I was finally able to let go of what Rex did to me. I realized that I am a strong, able woman, and I don't have to be a victim all my life. I'd like to thank you, Jan, for allowing me the opportunity for the beginning of my final cleansing. What a wonderful gift you gave me. Yes, you gave it to me. I might have thought it through in my shower, but you steered me in the right direction.

Thank You, Milli

Post Interview Letter:

Being part of this project has been an extraordinary experience for me. I have been telling my story for several years now, because I want battered women to have a voice and to give them hope and understanding. I also want others to truly understand that domestic violence can and does happen to anyone, anywhere. There are no social, economic or educational boundaries.

When this project began I knew I was going to be one of the first women interviewed and photographed. I work as a victim's advocate, and Jan wanted to be sure that this process would feel "safe" for other abused women. I was perfectly happy to be a "guinea pig," so to speak. I met Jan the previous winter and she told me that she was thinking of doing a book about abused women, focusing on the healing process that occurred in their bodies. She knew that most women who had been abused did not think of themselves as beautiful and she planned to do nude photographs that would show that all women are beautiful. I felt this was a wonderful idea and was happy to do whatever I could to help her. It never occurred to me at that time that I would be one of the women to be photographed. I felt I had done my healing long ago. And besides, nobody would ever want to photograph me nude.

When we did the interview, I realized that I had never really talked about the healing process, so this was a new experience for me. I could actually, physically, feel the healing again. I also realized that to a certain degree I would emotionally remove myself from my story when I told it. I often talked about being a survivor and the things I did to get out, but I hadn't done much talking about the things that actually happened to me while I was in that relationship.

As this project has grown, so have I. I am able to talk about things I have kept buried and was ashamed of. I discovered that I still had a lot of unresolved anger inside and have been able to voice my anger and know that it's OK.

Most of all, I now have a deep understanding that healing is an ongoing process and with each new experience that this project takes me to, I find I heal a little more and grow a little more.

What Happens to a Woman Battered

What happens to a woman battered?

Like a piece of fine fabric, that becomes torn and tattered.
Like a piece of fine china that is suddenly shattered.
Like the cloth and cup she will never be the same again.
She has been damaged, frayed and broken
Something beautiful has been lost forever.
But with care and kindness the right thread and glue
She can begin to repair the damage. She can begin to heal.

What happens to a woman battered when she begins to heal?

She becomes a quilt. She becomes a mosaic.
Beautiful in a new way and stronger than she ever was before.

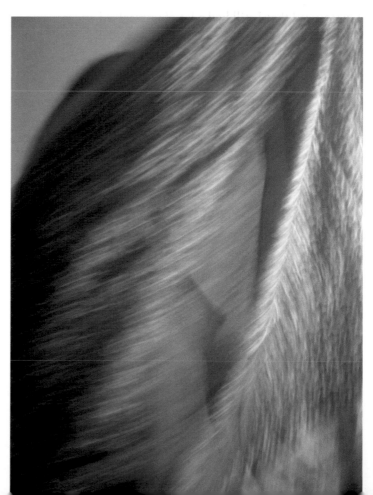

A.J.

"I began to feel healing in my hair and my neck. I had shoulder-length hair, and I lost it all due to nerves. After surgery I had a brace from neck to waist for four months. Now I've got my hair back, and a very tiny scar on my neck, and I'm extremely grateful. My life is good."

A.J. left her fifteen-year marriage with three daughters, a burst eardrum, fractured jawbone, concussion, and a herniated disk so close to her spinal cord they had to operate through the front of her neck.

"Now, I realize there was always verbal and emotional abuse, but we were married twelve years before he attacked me. We tried to make our marriage work through counseling, but when it happened again, I left. We were well-respected in the community, and he was a deacon at church. But I found out later, he was abused as a child, so it was learned behavior for him. We had our own business, a hundred thousand dollar income, a four bedroom home, Cadillac, boat and motorcycle. To leave all that and go to a shelter with my daughters was devastating."

In spite of this, A.J. pursued her bachelor's degree, graduating with The Dean of Students Returning Adult Student Award.

"I got a job with the Department of Justice, bought my own home and car, and put two girls through college. One more to go! My children have been so supportive, and we are very close. We've all been through extensive therapy and counseling, and it takes time. It took me three years to even admit I was angry, and that was an important step for me. You have to let yourself go through it all to get that healing, deep down inside."

A.J. feels that counseling and a support group is what helped her the most.

"After you leave, it's a struggle, and many women go back because it's so hard to do it on your own. So the most important thing is to connect with a support group; that is where you will get your strength, and realize you aren't alone. I went to my first support group and was shocked to see a former professor of mine; a beautiful, bright, blue-eyed, blonde woman whose husband was a prominent doctor in the community. People only see it happening to low income or women of color, but every day I see doctors, lawyers, women of every background."

"I was always a caring person, but since going through this, I really have empathy for other people, and I am grateful for that. I am the Aging Specialist for the Coalition Against Domestic Violence now, so I get to train advocates and police recruits across the state, and I have a real passion for it. When I work with women, I never tell them to leave, just give them the options and try to help them build their self-esteem back up so they can make their own decisions on what they need to. Once you're in a support group, you realize that no matter what color you are, or who you are, nobody deserves to be abused. Now, every time I share my story it brings me healing."

Migael

"In sailing, you use the wind to go forward, even when it's against you, and that's what helped me heal. My husband and I have lived on a boat since 1974, and a month after the rape, some friends came to visit. We took them sailing, and I discovered as soon as the boat left the dock, I could relax. I didn't have to be vigilant. It was very restorative."

In 1988, just returning to Seattle after four years on their boat in Alaska, Migael was raped at knifepoint in a laundromat on a busy street corner, in the middle of the day.

"There were two guys there when I put the clothes in, and when I came back after grocery shopping, there was only one. I was loading clothes in the dryer, when he came behind me with a knife, and forced me into the back room to rape me. He pulled my sweatshirt up over my head and strangled me. That was the worst part for me."

She tried everything to stop the attack, with no success. Then she remembered what she learned in Alaska—when you're attacked by a brown bear you play dead.

"I tried to calm down to get the knife out of my neck because I was bleeding. It worked to an extent, but when he strangled me, I thought I was dead. So I went limp and exhaled, and at that moment he let go of my neck. He said, 'You're a very lucky woman.' Then he left, but I'll never forget that chilling phrase."

Police arrived minutes after her call, but it was hours before she went home.

"It was a horrendous day, but in Seattle there is a lot of support, which makes a huge difference. Detectives and emergency room people are specially trained, and they helped me so much that day. They were one of the first to have a rape crisis center, too. I was oblivious to all of that, but thank God, when it happened to me, it was all there."

Information she gave them that day helped police find the rapist, six months later.

"I'm a writer, so when I was asked to describe him, I could do it, and that helped convict him. For mine and several other assaults, he went to prison for fourteen years. It's never enough years, but what felt good was that I had been heard; the whole community had acknowledged that this was wrong. This wasn't just a crime against me; it was against the whole community and the state. To have that outcome was fantastic, but not common."

Her healing began soon after the rape, coming in unexpected ways for many years

"I thought I'd be okay in about three months, but I felt worse after the numbness wore off. So I called the rape crisis center and talked to an advocate there every morning. Eight o'clock she'd call me. Sometimes that was the only thing that got me up. I think my healing began when I decided to write down every detail I could remember. I'd always kept a journal, and I started by describing what I could see and feel right now. I did that for years. The words helped me let it go a little bit, and even changed my nightmares."

Migael had made a living as a technical writer, but her personal writing yielded an unexpected gift three years later, when it became her first book, Still Loved By The Sun.

"I was functioning by then, but a piece of my spirit was still missing. I didn't have the range of joy or the sense of adventure I once had. You just do what's safe. So when I was invited to crew on a race in Alaska, I knew I had to go. It was my first race, I was the only woman on a six-person crew, and it was an incredible experience. I hope every survivor finds a way to do that, to go beyond the hanging-on period to finding joy."

Again her writing became the way she learned and continued to heal.

"I tried writing an article for a magazine, but the real story ended up being internal, and nobody wanted that. So I kept writing, and it took me a long time to discover what happened to me in that race. It's amazing how things come up in writing that you don't even know are there. Many years of writing and discovering became the book, *Back Under Sail*, in 2003."

Her trauma also provided a gift to other writers through her training for journalists.

"Mine was a high profile case, and I felt so harmed by the way one of the Seattle newspapers covered it. All the women in my support group said after they saw how the news media covered the story of my rape they would not report to police if it ever happened to them again. That is a very dangerous thing. So I wrote a letter to the editor and then was invited to talk to the news class at the University of Washington. That led to a collaboration with this incredible journalism professor, and since 1996 I have worked through their Dart Center for Journalism and Trauma. We help journalists learn to cover traumatic events with sensitivity, and all the little details that make such a difference to the victim. We also help them learn to pay attention to themselves because it is difficult for them as well.

"It was a horrible thing to go through, but so many good things have come from this. One person asked if I could change things, do I wish this had never happened to me? I said well, sure, except if I had to give back everything I had gained, it's a difficult question. All the incredible friendship and love I experienced, and everything good that came from it. I wouldn't want to give that back. The Migael Scherer you see today has been formed by all the things that have happened in my life, including this."

Cynthia

"I feel like my healing means just learning to be happy again. I lost all the dreams I once had, but now I feel free to do what I want, make my own decisions, and create new dreams. I can grow in my own way now." *Cynthia left with her four-year-old daughter when an emotionally abusive relationship turned violent.*

"He was still nice when we were dating, and I moved in with him when I got pregnant, so my child would have a father. After she was born, it was stressful. He was very controlling and there was a lot of mental abuse, yelling and threatening. I moved out, but when I went back, he became physically abusive after a very short time. At eleven at night, he told me to pack up everything and leave, and got my daughter up to watch. Then he wouldn't let me leave, and when I tried to take my daughter outside, he dragged me back in by my hair. He choked me and threatened to beat me up. My daughter was screaming and crying. She was very frightened and that's when I knew this needed to end."

She didn't call the police but she left the next day.

"I said I was going shopping and my daughter and I left and spent the night at a friend's house. The next day I went to HELP and they helped me with the process of placing a restraining order on him. They helped me see I could never change him, I could only change me."

Her support groups at HELP enabled her to look realistically at her relationship and begin healing.

"Now that I'm on my own, I can't believe I lived the way I did for five years. I always just thought I was with someone who wasn't perfect, and I could live with that. The healing came in realizing that I was in an abusive relationship and I needed to do something about it. I've come a long way, and I feel so free now."

Post Interview Letter:

Dear Jan,

Even though I kept my identity hidden throughout this project, I feel like I have exposed my true self to the world. Through this project, I have gained more confidence in my decisions about my life. I am not ashamed of my past. I am not perfect and people just need to accept me as I am.

Since doing this project I have created new dreams for the future. I have already fulfilled a few, with many more to come. It is hard to imagine the joy I feel now when I think about all I have accomplished.

I have come out of the shadows with the help of this project, friends and HELP. The healing process continues each day.

Everyone needs to remember how important their life is, and that no one has the right to take away your freedom of living without fear.

Cynthia

Linda

"He could do whatever he wanted to me, but he couldn't take my soul away from me or destroy my spirit. The traumatic impact of the physical violence is still there, but I can go within my spirit. As a Native woman, doing my spiritual practices on a daily basis is an important part of my healing."

Linda grew up with an abusive father, and met her husband when she was thirteen. She moved in with him at fifteen and abuse began immediately.

"I tried running away many times, but either he'd find me and bring me back, or I'd have to go back. I had no money and no place to live, and it's hard when you have kids. But every time I left, I got a little more courage."

She was finally able to divorce him when he went to prison—for raping her fifteen-year-old sister.

"There were four guys and he was one of them. I didn't know about it, but I knew something happened and when I asked her about it, she broke down. We filed charges and they all went to prison. Then I divorced him."

After prison and rehab, she thought he had changed, and they tried to make it work one more time.

"It was worse. Finally he tried to slit my throat and I thought I was dead. Somehow I got the knife away and stabbed him in the hand. This time I went to a shelter in another city. I couldn't let my kids witness that anymore."

The shelter was mostly Caucasian women, so it was difficult at first.

"But I talked to the staff and let them know what I needed to do for myself as a Native woman, and I was able to do that. I realized they are people who will support me, regardless of what happened. It's a fresh new start. In the support groups you get a lot of strength from each other, and I think that's a big part of the healing process too. It was a turning point for me and I'm grateful to them. They were really there for me."

Although she escaped the abuse, it has lasting effects on the entire family

"A drunk driver killed my son two years ago, and when I went through his things, I found all these poems. One was about growing up in an abusive family, how he hated it, and how he comes back when he's older and did the same thing that he swore he would not do.

"When my ex wanted joint custody I told the judge he put my son in a position to be exactly like his father, and that's what happened. I don't think the court systems look at that aspect. They look at the father's rights, but what about the kids' rights?"

Linda worked for a time as director of a domestic violence program.

"Being part of this movement gives me a lot of strength. I can help somebody else like others did for me. Maybe my experience can save someone else going through years of pain."

Heidi
with her daughter,
McKayla,
and her mom,
Lily

"A big part of my healing is being able to talk about it and not feel ashamed. I want to share my story with other teens so they don't feel alone."

Heidi

"If I had a magic pill that could change the past, I wouldn't, because I wouldn't have my daughter, and I can't imagine my life without her. My mom has been my rock, the backbone of my healing. Without her support I couldn't have done it. They have both been a big part of my healing."

Heidi's first experience with abuse was when she was a baby.

"My biological father was an alcoholic, and would get drunk, beat my mother, and then beat us. The night she left him he held us all at gunpoint. I was two, and she was nine months pregnant with my little sister. A year later she met a great guy, Mark, and he's always been my dad. They've been together twenty-six years, and he's a wonderful father."

When she was fifteen, Heidi was dating a twenty-year-old, and it turned ugly.

"I was very mature for my age, and always ended up dating older guys. This guy was never physically abusive, but always threatened me. He said if I ever left him, he'd kill me and kill any guy that came to my house. I was a size three and tiny, and had three teenage sisters, so that was a big threat. I could always talk to my mom about anything, so I don't know why I felt so isolated. I was scared, and at fifteen I decided I would rather be dead than live like this. At least then everyone else would be safe.

"So I broke up with him and he raped me. And he smashed his car into a tree. I didn't tell my mom about the rape, and probably never would have told anyone. He was the only guy I had ever been with, and I was ashamed and afraid. But I had to tell my mom when I found I was pregnant."

Heidi was still in high school, so she lived with her mom for the next two years.

"She was incredibly supportive, but also respectful that I was the parent. She helped me take him to trial, and it was like being raped all over again, but I had to do it. I feared he would come back to finish what he promised, so I wanted him in prison; but he only got three years probation since it was a first offense. I found out later he did watch our house, and even watched my daughter play in the yard; my biggest fear was he would hurt or kidnap her to get back at me. I've owned my own home for twelve years, but I still sometimes lay awake when I hear noises, paralyzed by fear that it might be him."

After the rape, Heidi didn't want anything to do with men, but destiny intervened.

"When I was five months pregnant, I met Ed and we became friends. We were the odd couple; I was fifteen and pregnant and he was twenty-three and a virgin. He was kind and loving and my life went forward in a positive way. We later married, and he adopted McKayla when she was four, but he was there since day one."

Heidi feels that being pregnant was part of what helped her heal.

"I think I might've dwelled on it more if I hadn't been pregnant, but I had this amazing little life to put my energy into. I never could have survived without support from my family, and feeling accepted and not judged by them.

"I always used to think of myself with my hands over my mouth, ashamed and afraid to speak out. A big part of my healing is being able to talk about it and not feel ashamed. I want to share my story with other teens so they don't feel alone."

Post Interview letter:

Before I did the interview for this project I didn't think I could ever tell McKayla about the rape. I struggled with whether or not to tell her because I am always honest with her. I knew I wasn't being honest and it ate me up inside, but I thought it would be too devastating for her. After talking to other women who took part in the project I decided to tell my daughter the truth. It was the hardest thing I've ever had to do. I was so afraid of her reaction and how it would affect her well being, but she took it really well. She is so strong. Even afterwards I wondered if I did the right thing, but then McKayla told me that she would rather know than not know, and she was glad I had told her the truth.

McKayla

"I don't know what to feel! I almost had the feeling like I was a mistake, but my mom says that I am not. I was really confused and didn't know what to think when my mom first told me, and I still don't know what to think. All I know is that I am thankful for such a great mom and such a great dad! Even though I don't know what to think about the whole thing I do know one thing, and that is that in my heart my dad (Ed) is my real dad and he always will be!"

Dolores

"My tears were the bleeding of my soul, my soul crying for healing. My heart and my spirit were broken, but my tears were like rain watering my soul to make it grow. I feel so lucky to be living where I do, surrounded by nature in the middle of a big city. I see new growth around me every day, and it reminds me to keep trying. My sadness was showing before, but now I feel my inner spirit shows on the outside too."

Dolores recently divorced her husband of nineteen years.

"About seven years ago, he started to be very controlling and manipulative, and doing what I call gaslighting. He would do things to make me think I was crazy. He became verbally and emotionally abusive, and started throwing things and pushing me a lot, then saying I made him do it. I should have seen that as a sign that the abuse was becoming more physical, but since he always told me everything that happened was my fault, I just kept trying to make it better."

Then one night he threw something at her, yelling, "You bitch!" and hit her in the leg. She knew she had to get out.

"I called the cops. But because I'm a compassionate person, I didn't have him arrested. That was probably a mistake, but I knew that it was beginning to escalate, and I paid attention to the sign this time."

Her husband continued to exert his control over her when she filed for divorce.

"He said 'Let the games begin. There's gonna be nothing left for you by the time we're done.' It's been difficult emotionally for me, because he's made it a nasty divorce. But going to therapy and joining the women's support group really helped.

"I am writing poetry again, and I joined a meditation group, and that really helps me sort things out. Looking back at my writings, I saw that in 1999 I wrote a poem about us coming apart. I could see this, but didn't realize until I looked back. I was in denial. Women need to go deep inside themselves and pay attention to their gut feeling. Now I'm just trying to get rid of that negative energy, and learn to stop blaming myself, as he did for so long. I am going deeper into my spiritual teachings, trying to learn from all this and become a positive person again."

Spiritual Healing

Our tears are the blood from our soul,
Streaming out of the body.
Released from the soul,
Letting go.
Through the tear ducts,
With which we were born.
The openings our soul knows
Where to bleed from

Nancy

"I was alone in this dark forest, and when I came out of the depression I could at last see light. I started hearing birds sing so loud, I couldn't imagine. I'd hear the wind rustling through the trees, and it's so loud, because for fifty years I didn't hear these things. The last two years I've been like a kid starting my life again. To hear those sounds, or notice flowers growing, and to smile and laugh—it's incredible."

Nancy suffered from depression and low self-esteem since childhood, and was involved in series of abusive relationships. She never recognized the depression until she came out the other side.

"I don't think I ever admitted how bad these relationships were until I started to feel better. I fell in love with a guy in college who was an alcoholic and verbally abusive. I started to explore the possibility of breaking up and went home to Madison overnight. I came back and he was drunk and accused me of going to see another man. He started hitting me and throwing me into the wall and the bathtub, just pounding my face, pulverizing me. I was scared. I thought, 'I'm not going to make it through this.' Thank God my roommate came home and was able to get him out.

"I went home for Christmas, all bruised and swollen, and my family was horrified. I stayed for three weeks, and said, "I still love him." I put up with it for two more years before I was able to leave."

But she went on to more bad relationships, and a date rape, her self-esteem in a continuous downward spiral. She married a very controlling man, and had two children. By the time she left him, she was on her way to incapacitating depression.

"I couldn't get out of bed, I couldn't eat, couldn't shower. I couldn't function at all, and had to quit work. After I attempted suicide, I was in a coma, on life support, for several days, and had to have a liver transplant. They gave me shock treatment, but it didn't help. They finally hit on a combination of five different drugs, and I started to feel better for the first time in my life. My partner was by my side through all of this, and even when I was one hundred ninety pounds, he thought I was beautiful.

"My dad suffered from depression, and finally committed suicide, so I worry about my kids, if this is hereditary. I go to schools and talk to other kids about depression as well. I suffered for so long, and I want to reach out to others, so they know they are not alone, and it *can* be treated. And I can give to myself now, too. I never knew it, but I am creative, and now I do art, crocheting and gardening all the time. I just feel like I'm really alive, and I appreciate life so much."

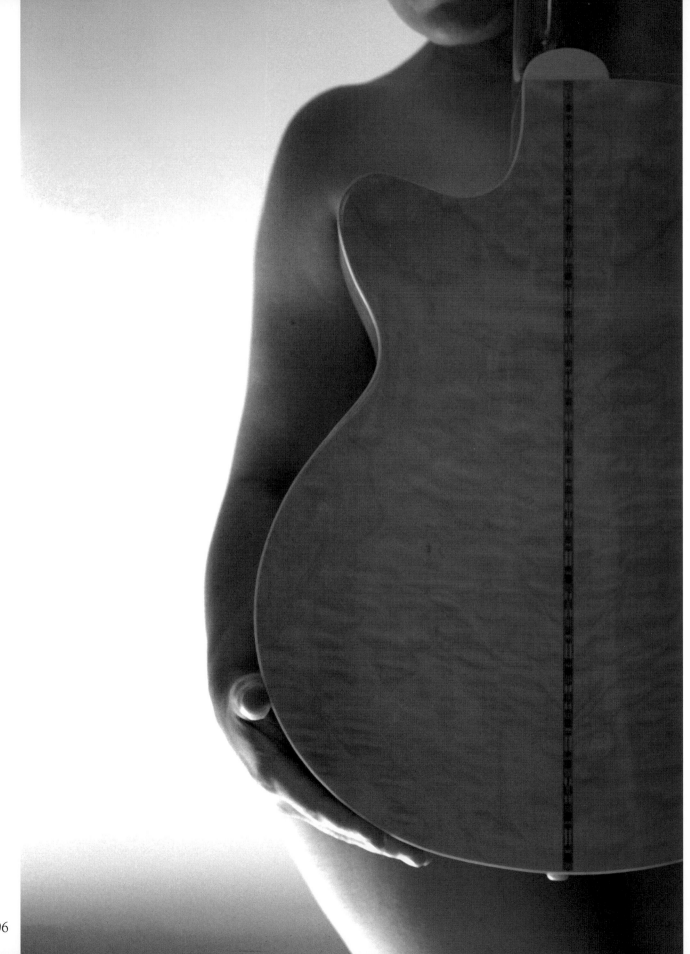

Jeanne K.

"At the age of fifty, I'm finally realizing my dream to perform and write my own music. I'm writing about my own experiences and my healing. The healing is this force coming out of my chest; my air, my essence. It enables me to tell my story in song, and to speak of painful things. It's so easy to go back to the place where I feel worthless, so each day I try to do something to remind me I value myself. I am also a painter, so every day I create something in paint or words or music that interprets the world I see, and the place my creativity was born from. The place I needed to heal from was rooted in guilt and doubt. It's easy to lose myself to others, so I must take time to remind me that I am important."

Jeanne first survived abusive marriages.

"I have been in several emotionally and sometimes physically abusive marriages. But in fairness to the men who have made my life miserable I'm sure I enabled them, because I allowed myself to be treated as an unimportant person and felt everything was my fault. I had lots of reasons to excuse why men treated me poorly. When I got knocked around, I thought, 'I'm strong enough to take it,' never admitting it wasn't normal. I was an ER nurse and I recognized signs of abuse in others, but it was hard to diagnose it as happening to me

"The father of my children was an evangelical Christian, and he 'saved me.' I spent years in this cult, convinced that I was nothing, God was everything, and women should be submissive to their husbands. I read a book called *A Chance to Die* and thought that as a little of my spirit died every day I was closer to God. When my husband left me for another woman, my feelings of worthlessness grew."

At forty-two she went to meet a man she had corresponded with since her divorce, and he raped her.

"It was a date rape. I had a bad feeling when I met him at the airport, but ignored it. I blamed myself and was embarrassed and angry I let it happen. I felt dirty, stupid, powerless and guilty, and had a whole list of things a forty-two-year-old woman should've done. I was always physically strong and had a red belt in *Tae Kwan Do*, so I was astonished by my immobility. I gave up and went inside my head. I was angry at myself—not him—for not being strong enough to stop him, and for even letting myself get into that situation. I couldn't forgive myself, and even lied to myself that it didn't happen. I awoke at night suffocating. When the next man I dated found out I'd been raped, he was convinced it happened because I really wanted it. It was demoralizing and confusing."

Seven years later, she was invited to sing at a gathering of women participating in this project.

"I realized I was one of them! I had no intention of talking about my experience, but I suddenly felt like I just had to tell someone, and there they were. My feelings of pain and inadequacy were reflected in their faces. They knew what I was talking about. After that I was able to talk about the rape with my new boyfriend, daughter and mother. They were wonderful. I had not allowed them the chance to be there for me, fearing what they might think of me. My boyfriend said that no matter how strong I was, there was always someone stronger. It's hard to forgive myself, but it helped me heal to know that what I've been through isn't wasted, and that I can help others understand. The lessons in my life are finally making sense. Talking with people who understand released me from my prison of self-hatred and doubt, and lightened the burden of carrying the sadness alone. Talking helped me learn about myself and how strong I could become. Verbalizing my feelings helped me define the abuse and make sense of chaotic thoughts."

Jeanne is learning to forgive herself and to love the beauty that was always there.

"I gained weight after the rape as protection, I think. If someone can see past the weight to the real me, I know they care about me. Our culture makes it difficult to feel beautiful if you don't fit the body types seen in the media. I feel more beautiful now from the inside out. I am learning to take care of myself and value friendships with women. The strength I see in women is amazing. I wrote a poem about women being like grass that grows through concrete. Women have this profound ability to nurture each other, heal each other. I am learning how to be feminine, vulnerable and strong at the same time. I'm really celebrating my life right now—all the things to come and all I've learned from what has happened."

Post Interview Letter:

It is really difficult to express how my life has changed since that first interview with Jan, and the photo shoot. So much has happened. I feel this flood of creativity has been set free because of the walls of guilt that have been knocked down. I feel new self-confidence and a new boldness in my life. I am not afraid of being alone. I am also not afraid of being loved and am more present in my relationships. My painting style and subjects have changed. I paint strong women: nudes, integrated with nature, rooted in Mother Earth. I am singing on my own, and the songs I write reflect a new sensitivity to the world around me and the people I see. I am not afraid to see the pain and to sing or paint about it. I am rejoicing in the strength of friendship and the healing abilities of the human spirit. I feel profoundly thankful that I have fallen in love with the women of this project; thankful for their willingness to share themselves for the good of others and for themselves. When I start drowning in the waters of my guilt and unworthiness, they are there to guide me back to fresh air.

I am awed by the events that Jan set into motion with her vision to document our healing. She jump-started this journey by asking me to focus on my healing instead of a night when I became lost to myself. And the performance . . . a night of cooperation between wounded spirits, daring to shine, opening up our intimate stories to family, friends and strangers, seeing faces shining with tears, and arms open with acceptance, filled that dark place in us. Jan offered me a place to start to speak, and my photo is a concrete image of a beautiful part of me that I can hold onto. I can breathe again. Thank you.

Sometimes in the Night

When I stand on a windy prairie
my arms reaching high
my body swaying to the rhythm of the earth
I am the grass
I bend but do not break
When I gaze up
at the red tail silhouetted against blue sky
I float
feel the loft of air under my wings
my hair streams out behind me
turns into feathers,
hands become talons.
I am the hawk
I am powerful

But sometimes at night
I wake up suffocating
my breath crushed out of my lungs
by memories of the weight of you that night
muscles meaningless in this panic

Sometimes at might
I wake up suffocating
my breath crushed out of my lungs by
this guilt

because I could not say no loud enough
could not fight hard enough
my strength useless before your assult
in the dark I lost my name.

Sometimes in the night
I wake up suffocating
my spirit weeping
because I gave up and hid inside my mind
I became powerless, powerless, powerless . . . .

But, when the earth turns again to the sun
I am the grass again
supple and bending, fractures gone
In this new dawn
I am finding myself again
breathing freely after speaking the unspeakable
dancing in the love of those who know me
healing slowly by the touch of gentle hands

Sometimes in the night
I wake up my hair turning to feathers
my hands strong as talons
and I am the hawk again
and I know my name

Sarah

"I felt like a beautiful flower, a really tight bud, and as I healed I began to open up, and the flowering began. Connecting with nature and Mother Earth is what saved me. I had no bonding or connection to my mother at all, so I needed to connect to earth in a deep way; I needed to feel her heartbeat."

In 1982, during an intensive bodywork session, she recalled sexual abuse by her father at age two, and early abuse and total rejection by her mother. At first she tried to deny the memories, tell herself she was making it up; but when shame over the incidents began welling up, she knew they were reality.

"The memory released the shame that had been locked in my body, and I knew it was real. The vivid memory of my father being drunk and rubbing me was traumatic, but even worse was my mother catching him and then beating on him while he was holding me, trying to protect me. She was yelling at him and calling me a little bitch. My mother was manic-depressive and alcoholic, and my father was also alcoholic, so there was always a lot of crisis and chaos in our family. My mother was in and out of mental institutions her whole life, and her rejection left me with a core belief that I was bad. I became a chiropractor to try and save my mother, though of course that was impossible. But it gave me greater insight and helped me begin my healing journey."

She has done deep healing work for over twenty years, and the family has done a great deal of work together.

"When I told my father what happened, it gave the others permission to begin their own journeys. Two years later all my sisters had memories resurfacing. My father never backed away, and took full responsibility for what he did. Eventually his own memories of being molested as a child came out, and I think that is usually where this comes from. He is eighty-three, and to see him have the courage to do this painful self-searching is really beautiful. I have such honor and respect for that. That's the freedom—getting to a place of forgiveness. It's a journey I'll probably be on at some level the rest of my life.

"To look at the level of trauma and the survival capacity of the human spirit, and to see how my family members have evolved and grown is such a gift. I would not change a thing in my life. I embrace my life as it is. It's time to just be, and to let my heart be wide open and be the most beautiful me I can be. That's how we heal—we just help each other along."

Gay

"When I was beginning my healing process and my therapy around the abuse issues, I had wonderful dreams. I'd be flying way above things, and it was great as long as I believed in myself and my ability to fly. When I got scared in the dream, I brought myself down. It was just like in my life. That feeling of being free, letting go of fear, and believing in me is what I keep working towards now."

A few years ago, at age forty-three, in a therapy session for unrelated issues, Gay had body memories of being sexually abused by her maternal grandmother.

"I felt the memory in my vagina and I knew immediately it was my grandmother. She was mentally ill, married seven times, and her last husband abused me as well. I started hyperventilating, thinking of my siblings; had this happened to them as well?"

Once she began to have the memories, she wanted to uncover everything.

"Part of it was to feel like I had some control, and part of it was wanting to be done with it, which of course you never really are. I spent the next year in therapy crying and grieving, but also finding a lot of things that had always bothered me now made sense. Like I've always had a very hard time relaxing and letting go at night, and I found it was connected to my grandmother coming in and molesting me while I was sleeping. I never knew if she was bad or just nuts, but I sensed her power in a really icky way. I've been divorced four times, and I worry I may be like her. But finding out what happened to me has helped me understand why I do the things I do in relationships. I've always come from a place of powerlessness, doing what other people wanted me to do, regardless of what I want. That may stem from the abuse, and it has caused a lot of problems in my life. It's how I ended up getting married the last time, caving in to what he wanted. He's a great guy, but I have at last been able to stand up for myself and say I don't want to be married. It was a big step for me. As painful as the memories are, it was kind of a relief . . . now I can gather up all the parts of me and own myself. I can finally own all of who I am."

One of the things she had to relearn in healing was the simple act of breathing.

"I'd often feel unable to breathe; I felt pressure on my chest and I discovered it was connected with my grandma's husband being on top of me, though I don't believe he ever penetrated me. To overcome this, I took voice lessons; I'd cry when my voice teacher was trying to show me how to breathe and I couldn't do it. But it eventually worked. So then I took scuba lessons. I had major panic attacks and quit, but was finally able to snorkel—and loved it! It was a major accomplishment to face that fear and be able to breathe normally."

She feels as if she's always had two lives—one conscious, and one unconscious.

"It was like a split personality; part of me was holding and repressing those memories, acting from that viewpoint, but the rest of me didn't know it. When kids are threatened that they will be hurt or killed if they tell, they bury it so deep, and the shame is implanted. I'm working on bringing those two lives together, and being by myself helps me with that; I can be more present, and more aware of how I'm feeling. We all heal at our own pace, and I have to remind myself to respect that and respect myself.

"I'm trying to take care of the child in me who was so damaged. Balancing parenting myself, and parenting my son has been difficult. He's angry with me for getting divorced, and I feel like a sponge absorbing his pain. I have to forgive myself for hurting him and honor my own progress. Being able to stand up for what I need, and becoming real before his eyes is huge, but sometimes it's terrifying to let go of my old way of being.

"My mantra is, 'I'm doing the best I can, and my best is good enough.' When I say that and then start to cry, I know I'm being too hard on myself, and I need to lighten up."

Adell and Sheila

Adell

"**M**y vision of healing is to be surrounded by women celebrating life, and it would have to include Sheila. I've known Sheila since I was about ten, and she was my rock through all of this. She helped me be strong enough to leave, and maybe my leaving gave her strength, too."

Adele married when she was twenty-one, and the physical abuse began six months later.

"The first time, he hit me in the eye with a closed fist and it required seven stitches. I was ashamed and embarrassed. Being a newlywed, it was hard to explain having two black eyes, so I told people at work I was in a car accident. A couple months later it happened again and I got nine stitches in the top of my head. This time I think they knew."

She was married seven years, and the abuse continued the entire time.

"When I had injuries, I would isolate myself, and that was part of his power and control over me; isolate me so my family didn't know and couldn't encourage me to leave. My self-esteem was on the ground. But at about six years, I knew I had to get out. I had gotten a job in an alcohol and drug unit, and that started to enlighten me. He often threatened to kill me if I left him, and when I learned how alcohol affects a person, I knew it could really happen. The abuse was getting worse and it was just a matter of time."

So one Sunday she put some clothes in a bag, telling him she was doing laundry at her mother's house. She took her son, and left with no intention of returning.

"He was amazed when I told him I was leaving. After a few days of calls didn't get me back, he came by, and when I wouldn't talk to him, he broke out windows. I called the police but they couldn't touch him because it was not mandatory then to arrest a man on a domestic violence call. Today it is. So he kept it up, and after a couple months of this I got a restraining order. At that time you had to pay for restraining orders, but now they are free for domestic violence. So after I got the order, he kept coming and they finally caught him. He spent nine months in jail because of the property damage he did. While he was there I filed for divorce."

Adele now helps other women gain the strength to make life-changing decisions.

"I don't think life could be better now. I own my own home, I work in a domestic violence shelter, and I feel like I'm making a difference in the lives of women who are in the same situation I was in. That has helped my own healing a great deal. Without having gone through that I wouldn't be where I am today. It truly makes me grateful."

Sheila

"I think Adell and I saved each other. We've been friends since we were children and she has always been such a beautiful person to me, inside and out. I was there when she went through her trauma and she was there for me. Our healing process has been helping each other."

Sheila was one of ten children, and in her mid-twenties memories of sexual abuse by her two older brothers began to surface. She struggled to dismiss them.

"I went to a therapist then, but whatever she said scared me, so I didn't go back. I was into protecting my family, and convincing myself it wasn't true, so my healing process didn't begin until five years later. I work in counseling and knew of a therapist who specialized in working with women of color, so I made an appointment to—I thought—talk about my ex-boyfriend, being hurt again and not trusting men. But it was all about my childhood. It wasn't only the sexual abuse, but there was verbal and physical abuse from my mom as well. I learned later that four of us had been abused by the same two brothers. I was angry at my mom for not stopping it, but realize now she was doing the best she could at the time. My therapist was wonderful, and helped me understand how the abuse and the things I couldn't control as a child have formed some unhealthy decisions I made as an adult, and that I can change that. It was a spiritual awakening."

During this time Sheila and Adell helped form a sister group of twenty-five African American women, from homemakers to executives with Masters Degrees. They met once a month to help each other through whatever life gave them.

"That was a tremendous part of my healing, and has been one of the best things to happen to any of us. We'd each write a question and put it in a basket, then you'd pick one and address the concern your sister had from your frame of reference. It's not twenty-five anymore, but the core group has been together over twenty years, and we still help each other. We've been through everything together, the traumas and the joys."

Sheila found her way back to the church and the God she had been so angry at, and made a decision to move on in her life, and to focus on her blessings.

"I was explaining over and over how I had been abused, and that was a way for me to hide out and stay in the victim role. As long as I decide to play the victim, that's the role I'll be stuck in. I'm not just a survivor either. God has healed me, and blessed me, and now I get to help other women heal as well."

Karen

"It was so healing to be there; just the water and the quiet. Nature was the perfect space to put myself in, and the ocean, in particular has always been the place I go to for healing. I refused to let those two men ruin my love affair with that island, which was such a magical, spiritual place for me."

Karen was in Jamaica just three days when two men raped her.

"The friends I was visiting were renting an abandoned coconut plantation, and when we came back that evening, I could sense the ominous presence of someone when we walked through the door. They were hiding in the shadows. They had guns. They tied up my three male friends and ignored the Jamaican woman with us. I was the only white woman, and they took me hostage. They first raped me by the pool, then made me drive them into the hills. All the while I had a gun on my forehead, and another at the back of my head, as they argued with each other about some curfew. As terrified as I was, I knew I had to pay attention so I could find my way back. Soon they yelled at me to stop the car. They threw me down on the backseat and then on top of the car, each of them taking their turn with me, with a knife at my throat and a gun at my head the whole time. They were yelling at each other as they penetrated me. It was so impersonal, as if I didn't even exist. I was so afraid of the gun and knife that I dared not move, but my entire inner being twisted and struggled with all its might. Then something happened inside of me and I surrendered. I stopped resisting and just let go. I immediately found myself outside my body, witnessing without pain or panic what was going on below. The minute I did that, it was over. They put me in the car and I somehow got back to the plantation. A young man who worked at the estate slept outside my door every night after that, but I never for one moment felt safer. The idea that anyone could protect me was gone forever."

She was visiting Jamaica after selling her business in Toronto to move to Los Angeles with her boyfriend, and continue work in the music business.

"I called my boyfriend and told him what happened. When I arrived in Los Angeles a few days later, he told me he was involved with another woman and had given her all my clothes I'd shipped ahead. And the owner of the record label I was going to work for had just died of a cocaine overdose. My head was spinning. I could hardly believe the intensity with which life was trying to get my attention. I was walking into a world of coke and craziness, but my heart was pulling me in another direction. I decided to go back to Jamaica and spent the next year living on the secluded cliffs at the west end of the island. I studied myself in a way that one only can when time has slowed down. I spent hours every day by the ocean, slowly unraveling the inner workings of my psyche as I came to understand the significance of the recent events. Both the rape and the events in Los Angeles felt like life was tapping me on the head—'Wake up, Karen.' I spent time alone, meditated, wrote daily and slowly healed."

Healing allowed her to follow a new path in her life. Intensive training as a massage therapist brought self-discovery that would help others heal.

"I used to sing a lot, but after the rape, I stopped. A voice teacher shared with me that my throat was closed up, and I immediately felt the knife at my throat and not being able to yell. Bodies habitually tense as a way to protect if they have been violated. Because of my own personal experience, I'm very sensitive to this, so therapists often refer people to me who have been physically or sexually abused. Safe, non-sexual bodywork can help people who have been traumatized to re-frame the experience of touch, allowing them to relax their vigil and experience themselves in an incredibly healing way. I was fortunate that I was twenty-nine when I was raped and had positive sexual relations before; I did not confuse rape with the sexual act. Children and women who have not experienced loving sexual contact have a much more difficult time."

Karen also realized she was in no way responsible for the rape.

"Nor did I feel any guilt or shame, but I knew that I *was* responsible for what I did with the experience afterwards. I knew that choice would determine the quality of the rest of my life. I can never erase that night from my history; it's a part of what has shaped me. I don't identify myself by it though, and it doesn't lead my life. If I choose to see myself as a victim, I relinquish all power to those men, and I would never turn my personal power over to anyone, especially someone acting out of fear and powerlessness themselves.

"One of the most important insights I gained that night is how strong I am internally. I know that nothing can destroy me because I now recognize that I am more than my body. I know there is no way my energy and my soul can be destroyed, so no matter what anyone does to my body, they have no power over me. That's how I was able to surrender that night, and the minute I did that, my attacker literally jumped off me. In the moment, I didn't understand the profoundness of that.

"I believe that healing is a journey, and that I have to be willing to let go of the goal or the result, and just enjoy the 'trip,' the 'now,' the process of getting to know myself, becoming intimate and trusting with myself. If I want to see change in my life, I have to be willing to make some change in me. I'm thankful for the healing and for the learning and strength that has come from this experience; I say prayers of gratitude all the time for the blessings that have been bestowed on me.

"Meister Eckhart once said, "If the only prayer you ever prayed was *Thank You*, that would be enough.""

Sandra

"Flamenco is like a religion to me. It's not God, but when I step onto the dance floor, I am in prayer and adoration for life. I jump in like a leap of faith. Centered, I am in power (empowered) and in spirit (inspired). This spirit we call *Duende*, but I believe it is the Holy Spirit. Flamenco has always spoken to me, and allowed me to understand the mysteries of life; this is what has helped me to heal. As I dance I can feel myself open, and my heart can communicate and interact."

Sandra's passions were repressed for many years in an abusive relationship.

"When I was sixteen I met a guy who was idolized by everyone, including me. I didn't think I was pretty or smart or built, so when this popular senior asked me out I felt I had to do anything to keep him. I see now that was a pivotal decision. I gave up who I really was."

She got pregnant, they married, and he soon became very jealous and controlling.

"I tried to improve myself; I wanted to be a great woman and I guess he felt threatened. He would try to control me and when I talked back, he'd hit me. I got hit all the time. I stood by him because I loved him and felt guilt about him being only twenty and having to work and support us. I thought overlooking his bad temper was a way of loving him, but I was trying so hard to be 'good' and still I would 'get him mad.' I started to realize there was something very wrong, even sick, with our relationship. Maybe I really didn't deserve this abuse. I was exhausted and sometimes admitted to things I didn't do just to get the fight over with. The kids, too, were showing signs of stress, like nightmares, nervous stomach, headaches that went on for months, and jumpiness at sudden noises.

"I first sought help when we got into an argument in the car; he grabbed me by my neck and hit my head against the window and punched me in the head. I had been pushed against the wall, kicked between the legs and slugged many times, but to get yanked by the neck seemed more threatening and demeaning to me, so I went to an emergency room. I wasn't bleeding but I was so shaken up that I was searching for help. When the doc asked what happened, I said my husband hit me. To hear myself admit this to a professional was both embarrassing and self-awakening. When he said, 'He shouldn't do that'—a light went on. The doctor didn't ask, like most people had before, what I had done to make him mad. He simply said he shouldn't do that, and reached for some pamphlets and information on domestic violence and support groups."

She began reading self-help books and attending meetings, trying to find herself again.

"Armed with doctors orders, I now had hope. I was still isolated but I could read, although I had to do it behind his back. Anything I did that helped me to grow or change was so threatening to him, and he'd try and interfere or stop me. He was afraid to face his own demons and inner pain. We tried counseling, but the abuse continued."

After four children and fifteen years, she was finally able to leave for good.

"The last two years of our relationship we were separated; he was having an affair and I had my own apartment, but he still considered me his woman. Now there was also sexual, financial and emotional abuse. And he'd accuse me of cheating, shaking out my purse for evidence of my disloyalty, and slapping me around. Finally, I left everything, packed the kids and went to another city. I felt so different; very scared, but like there was a sad victory. I started singing *Amazing Grace* every time I got behind the wheel."

They lived in her car for two weeks, until the sheriff helped her get into a shelter.

"Everything that happens in the spirit of support is so precious. I'll never forget the transformation that took place at the shelter. I had so much guilt, taking the kids from their father; they missed him and loved him, and it was very confusing. I saw how quickly they bounced back and forgave, and I knew their beauty did not deserve the life we had made for them. I had to rise up to them. They were so willing to be joyful and loving despite what we put them through; they woke me up! Once we were in the shelter, we could rebuild our lives. We were in an atmosphere of recovery, even if the showers were cold and the food was from a can. We will always be grateful to the families and the staff of that shelter. My kids have been the light of my life, just like angels. Children are great teachers if you listen, and if you're open."

When she moved to San Francisco, she again found support through a group.

"I connected with La Casa de Las Madres when I was searching for a surgeon to work on my nose, broken from the violence. What I found was caring and support to help heal a broken family. I'm amazed at what comes from acceptance, awareness and compassion. La Casa has made a huge positive impact in the lives of entire families.

"I have absolutely nothing against men, but everything against cruelty and violence, which is, I believe, largely due to ignorance and fear. I want to keep building on the strength and inner guidance I have discovered within myself. I'm learning to honor my self and not be afraid to speak up. And to live up to the challenges of conscious living, social justice, and personal freedom.

"La Casa had an art project where we decorated shoes to tell a story about leaving our abusive situation, and healing. I chose ruby slippers. I thought about how we sometimes spend our lives desiring something we already have within us. The character of the Wicked Witch in Oz was seen as evil, and I too once thought of myself as wicked and bad. The desire to be free is what it's all about. Maybe the witch wasn't evil after all—and neither am I. Maybe she was just fighting for something that was rightfully hers. I think that is what I've discovered about myself too."

Post Interview Letter:

For that moment when I was open to being photographed, I experienced freedom. Sweet delicious, freedom. To me it was freedom from my own fear in the form of judgmental thinking. The thoughts of lack and worthiness; That I'm too this, or too that.

These thoughts are not Truth!

The truth is I'm alive and I have a lot of love to share.

This is my truth.

I realized this truth as I felt my own joy. With seemingly nothing to be joyous about, I felt joy!

I opened up, naked to the world. And for those moments I was not afraid. I moved to the core statements of my soul.

Women in Shadow and Light

To feel the chilling air, and have a natural relationship with the world; To hug a tree and not feel worry. To stretch my arms and reach for humanity—This I love, this my life!

A natural relationship to the world.

A natural woman.

I now know I can choose this freedom again. What a relief to be your true self; To Be— Soulfully, aware of your own presence—Life.

Freedom – what a turn on!

Thanks, Jan!

Love, Sandra

Sandra wrote a poem about what flamenco means to her and to her healing:

The call sounds like a dream; a dream too good to be true—
You have to read between the lines, see the unseen,
forgive the unforgivable—
See your reflection, the unrest, the passion—
Face even the darkest times, the poverty, the death of the ego
Prepare to lose it all and surrender—
Be brave and open—
Open to receive this your call—
And with all your heart and all your soul recognize,
here within you,
a taste of heaven on earth.

Gayle

"Water and light are so healing to me, especially moonlight. I feel good about my body in water, like I don't have to hide behind the veil of shame."

Gayle lived with shame and guilt since two incidents of sexual abuse cast a shadow over her self-image. At age five, a male cousin molested her. At sixteen, still a virgin and just after losing a significant amount of weight, she was raped by three boys while on a first date with one of them.

"That changed my whole perception of my self-worth. I had so much shame and guilt about my poor choice going out with him, so I never told anyone. I suppressed it in humiliation, as a matter of survival. I gained weight back and hid under baggy clothes. I lived in a paradox of wanting to be desired, but not allowing myself to be attractive."

When Gayle began therapy five years ago for unrelated issues, her therapist questioned whether her eating compulsion was relative to any sexual abuse. At first she wanted to deny it, but began realizing the connections between the two. She was surprised that some of the rape details had been successfully suppressed for years, but as memories of the rape resurfaced, she dealt with them, identifying and addressing the shame and guilt.

"I had buried it for so long that the denial was reality to me. But then it was right in my face and I had to figure out how to deal with it. Coincidentally, that night after therapy, I was meeting two girlfriends from high school. I decided to tell them I was raped, because it was a guy they knew. It turned out something similar also happened to one of those women, so I got a lot of support. I told the right people and it triggered the beginning of my healing."

She said felt an immediate change in her persona, and began losing weight, dressing, walking and talking differently.

"The veil I was hiding behind lifted. I found it was not the sexual abuse I had to heal, it was the shame. I could forgive those boys for what they did, but then I had to learn to forgive myself and heal the shame. That was the core issue. The real damage wasn't the physical violation to my body; it was the damage to my self-worth. I saw myself as unworthy of sincere intimacy. The shame I felt toward myself blocked me from fully accepting love and intimacy.

"When the shame was recognized and addressed, forgiveness and healing became possible. After thirty years of hiding my shame, I was released; I blossomed as a woman for the first time in my life."

Post Interview Letter:

Dear Jan,

A year has passed since we toured Door County, attempting to find some privacy in moonlight. It was an experience full of stories to last me well into old age. Being able to laugh in the nude! What a concept for me, after hiding for all of those years. As I was riding my bike in the nude down that mosquito-ridden wooded road, I couldn't help praying that I wouldn't fall. I didn't want to explain to the doctor why I had gravel on my bum!

I want you to know that my involvement in this project unexpectedly became an extension of my healing. The project brought me into a community of other victims, but more than that, into a community of women healers, self-healers. There was a sense of power in those women, and I was one of them! Together we were even more powerful. And definitely more powerful than our perpetrators.

I took my daughter and son to the exhibit, hoping the impact would educate them and open the possibility of communication. It was difficult for my son, at first; he was expecting it would be a girly show. When he realized there was dignity in the photographs, he got into them, but with confusion about why I was part of the exhibit. Suddenly he got it, and it opened up an opportunity for us to discuss date rape and the importance of respect toward girls.

As a result of the experience, I feel closure. My experiences no longer feel like issues; they are simply another part of my history, the history that evolved me into the woman I offer the world today.

Thank you, Jan

Sincerely, Gayle

Water

Water
I soar through cleansing water
Purifying my dirt
Purging thoughts of yesteryears
So sticky with shame.

Water
A silky slinky veil
Untangles my tendrils of fear
Opening my flesh to its moist caress
Inviting my pleasure.

It was with my own life force
I traveled through my cave of shame
Trust abandoned at the cave's mouth
I groped through the darkness fatigued
Propelled by the dream of you
Fluid like cleansing water
You in moonlight
At cave's end.

Often weary
I'd rest in my journey
Contemplating consequences of a search abandoned
The dream of moonlight coaxed me on.

The moon I trusted
Even in darkness
Constant, loyal
Lighting my path with a subtle silent smile
No explanations, expectation, inquisitions
No forcing my heart closed, my knees open
I was not here to satisfy him
So I continued
Seeking his light
Light of trust
Searching the cleansing water
Renewed life.

And it was with my own life force
I entered water's fresh abyss—fully exposed
With flexed fervor
I plunged through water's succulence
Abandoning the dirty past of Shame's darkness
Surfacing with my first gasp of cleansing breath
And there you stood
Offering me Moonlight.

Water
A silky slinky veil
Untangles my tendrils of fear
Opening my flesh to its moist caress
Inviting my pleasure.

Ellie

"I'd like to hold out hope to other women . . . to let them know they aren't alone; they aren't the only ones these things happened to, and they can survive. They can get through it, and get their soul back."

Ellie was sexually and physically abused by her mother from about age four. When she was twelve, her uncle began sexually abusing her.

"That was the only physical contact I had with my mother, because she did not cuddle or show other affection. So when she told me it was OK, I believed her. When I got older and said no, she became violent and abusive, and tried to kill me several times. She said it was my fault and I was evil, so I had to die. I believed my whole life that I was evil, until I got into therapy. I had no one else to turn to, and I fragmented—I split into three personalities. It was the way I survived. I sort of adopted my aunt as my mother, but then when my uncle began to abuse me I'd dissociate, I'd just go away."

Ellie married young, seeing this as her chance to escape, and became pregnant immediately. She never told her husband about the abuse.

"Being pregnant was very scary; I cried a lot. But I had made a conscious choice when I was twelve years old that I would never ever do that to a child. My children and their children will never go through that."

She raised her children, never telling anyone her 'horrible secret.' At age fifty, with her children grown, Ellie could no longer repress the memories and was hospitalized when she became suicidal.

"I felt like I could shatter into a million pieces that would never go back together. The defense system I'd built fell apart and it was terrifying, but I knew I had to face the truth or kill myself. It sent shock waves through my family, and my husband felt betrayed that I hadn't told him, so there were times we didn't know if we'd make it. Plus I had to fight the attitude of society that mothers don't abuse their children in this way. But they do. What kept me going was a belief that my purpose in life was to stop this, and not have it continue through my children and their children."

Ellie still suffers physical, as well as emotional, consequences of years of stress and abuse. She has a brain lesion from an old injury, and had bypass surgery for what she calls her 'broken heart.' She's had over ten years of psychotherapy, and has become a strong and positive force.

"That repeated abuse does change your brain chemistry, and I will always be working on the healing. But I have a lot of respect for that little girl I was; I survived without going mad. It was a fight to integrate into a whole woman, but I did it. I've been able to forgive my mother; she was mentally ill, and no one would help her or even acknowledge her bizarre behavior. It's harder to forgive my father for not doing anything.

"Being in nature, just being out in that beauty and goodness takes me out of myself and helps me to heal. Being part of this project has been the most healing of all. I have always hoped I could be a vehicle of healing for

Brooke

"When I saw this exhibit, I felt these women were speaking directly to me. They helped me see what happened to me in a new way, and release the pain I had stored for seven years. That deep connection allowed me to speak about that incident for the first time. Releasing the shame has given me a real sense of strength and joy. I feel empowered by owning my experiences. Now I want to bring that same honesty into my relationship with my daughter and to pass this inner strength I feel to her. I can teach her the lessons I've learned, help her feel strong in who she is and share my joy with her."

Brooke emerged from a time of teenage rebellion with many experiences she wanted to forget.

"I thought I was being so and independent. I ran away from home and was headed down a self-destructive path. When I was only sixteen, there was a very traumatic incident that I minimized by saying I was 'taken advantage of.' I was in denial. Instead of putting blame where it belonged—on the boy—I blamed myself: I shouldn't have been drinking; I should have known better; I should have fought harder."

Afraid of bringing shame to her parents, and unsure if anyone would believe her, she kept this secret to herself.

"I clumped those experiences and my poor choices as a teen into 'the past,' content that I had been able to learn from my mistakes. It was part of what shaped me, but not who I was. I moved forward in my life, never daring to admit even to myself what really happened, but convinced I had dealt with the issue sufficiently."

Seven years later, she began to see that the pain was still locked inside her.

"I'd just left an emotionally abusive relationship, and was enjoying being on my own and getting to know myself for the first time in my life. I went to visit my aunt and see the exhibit and performance of *Out of the Shadows*, knowing the subject matter, but completely unprepared for my reaction. As I wandered among the photographs and read the stories of these brave women, all of my repressed emotions came bubbling up and overflowed into the tears streaming down my cheeks. My wound was opened. I felt confused and scared of my feelings. These women—some older and some younger than me, but all with like bodies, souls, hearts and stories—spoke to me. They shared their pain for the world to see, so they could help themselves and reach out to people like me. When Jan came into the room and saw my tears, she hugged me, and for the first time, I allowed myself to say these painful words: I was raped."

She began therapy the very next week.

"My body stored the memories until I was ready to deal with the pain. I see how the rape has affected every relationship I've had since then, but I can forgive myself now, and know I'm worthy of a healthy loving relationship. I know that everyone has the ability to heal, and also to help someone else heal. These brave women—Jeanne, Kathy, Gayle, Ellie, all of them—showed me I was not alone. They opened their lives so all victims of abuse could become survivors, and helped me begin my own journey. Being able to talk about this publicly is a huge step in my own healing, and I know that one day I will be able to help someone else to heal too. It is the least I can do."

Epilogue

We are each a tapestry, woven of the dark shadows of our past as well as shiny golden threads of light. Until we step into the light, we cannot see our shadow, and it is only when we can embrace them both that we become whole.

This book is a celebration of wholeness and healing, shadow and light, courage and strength. It is a celebration of women who are survivors of abuse, but mostly they are just beautiful, ordinary, extraordinary women. They have stepped out of the shadows to share their light to help others to find their way.

National Center For Victims of Crime

Information on a wide range of topics to increase awareness of the consequences of victimization and the options and resources available to help victims. This information is designed to compliment and enhance the services of victim service professionals. If you need referrals to local victim service providers, call 800.FYI.CALL (800.394.2255). http://www.ncvc.org

The Brazos County Rape Crisis Center

Based in Texas, this unique site offers anonymous confidential counseling. You can send an anonymous message and receive a reply within 24-72 hours. http://rapecrisis.txcyber.com

Parents and Loved Ones of Sexual Abuse and Rape Survivors

A comprehensive site that offers information and tips. http://www.geocities.com/HotSprings/2656

Healing After Abuse, Incest, Rape, Assault

After you have been a victim of rape, incest, domestic violence or sexual assault, there are many ways to begin the healing process. Learn about therapy, relaxation techniques, the legal system, and help available at crisis centers. http://incestabuse.about.com/cs/healing

Laura Davis (Laura D.), author of *The Courage to Heal, I Thought We'd Never Speak Again* and several other books on incest survivors and healing, offers an excellent site. http://www.lauradavis.net

Feminist.com

This is a ten-year-old activist community and consciousness-raising portal of resources and information that supports women's equality, justice, wellness and safety. http://www.feminist.com

VDay

This is a global movement to stop violence against women and girls, started by Eve Ensler, author of *The Vagina Monologues*. VDay is a demand: Rape, incest, battery, genital mutilation and sexual slavery must end now. V-Day is a spirit: We believe women should spend their lives creating and thriving rather than surviving or recovering from terrible atrocities. http://www.vday.org

Center for the Prevention of Sexual and Domestic Violence

This website contains information about the intersection of religious issues and child abuse, domestic violence, sexual abuse and clergy misconduct. http://www.faithtrustinstitute.org

Women in Shadows and Light is available at your favorite bookstore or on-line. Bulk quantities may be purchased directly from the publisher at Beagle Bay Books, 775.827.8654; 775.827.8633 (fax); sales@beaglebay.com.

For information on ordering *Out of the Shadows* performance videos, CDs by Jeanne K with songs related to this project, and all other inquiries about the exhibit or to schedule Jan Goff-LaFontaine to speak to your group or store, please go to www.janlafontaine.com